100 GREATEST
Sports Cars

BY THE AUTO EDITORS OF CONSUMER GUIDE®

Publications International, Ltd.

Louis Weber, C.E.O.
Publications, International, Ltd.
7373 North Cicero Avenue
Lincolnwood, Illinois 60646

Manufactured in U.S.A.

8 7 6 5 4 3 2 1

ISBN: 0-7853-1960-3

Library of Congress Catalog Card Number 96-71796

*I*f enthusiasts argue over what constitutes a sports car, imagine how they debate what makes a great sports car. Answers to both questions involve the tangible and the emotional.

In the beginning, a sports car was a roadster—an open two-seater with a detachable soft top and side curtains. Its purpose was pure driving fun, and it was capable of participating in motorsports with little modification. What most Americans think of as sports cars appeared after World War II, when GIs brought home MGs and other British models.

Those delicate lightweights couldn't match the acceleration of American V-8s. They had rock-hard suspensions, abbreviated weather protection, and were noisy. But their nimble handling was a revelation to Yanks weaned on clumsy Detroit iron. And their long-hood/short-deck proportions, snug seating for two, and jaunty wire wheels celebrated this new way of motoring.

By the 1960s, sports cars were shedding their crude simplicity. The "race and ride" ideal was less viable, and buyers demanded amenities. Open models got windows, and there was a proliferation of closed body styles. But what was true then is true now: Be it a four-cylinder ragtop or an air-conditioned V-12 coupe, it's not a sports car unless it's primary role is driving fun.

CONTENTS

PHOTOGRAPHY
The editors gratefully acknowledge the cooperation of the following people who supplied photography to help make this book possible. They are listed below, along with the page number(s) of their photos:

Sam Griffith: Front cover. **Chan Bush:** 6; **Peggy Dusman, American Automtive Manufacturer Association:** 8; **Mike Mueller:** 9; **Nicky Wright:** 10, 15, 32, 33, 66, 67, 90, 91, 94, 95, 157, 158, 159, 162, 163, 202, 203; **Doug Mitchel:** 11, 26, 27, 38, 65, 39, 82, 83, 116, 117, 122, 123, 182, 183; **Joseph H. Wherry:** 11, 13, 14; **David Gooley:** 13, 20, 21, 22, 23, 98, 99, 104, 105, 110, 111, 112, 113, 214, 215; **Vince Manocchi:** 14, 16, 17, 18, 19, 24, 25, 36, 37, 44, 45, 46, 47, 52, 53, 57, 60, 61, 62, 63, 64, 65, 68, 69, 70, 71, 72, 73, 74, 75, 78, 79, 96, 97, 106, 107108, 109, 118, 119, 128, 129, 138, 139, 148, 149, 150, 151; 160, 161, 165, 166, 167, 178, 179, 186, 187, 188, 189, 190, 191, 198, 199, 200, 201, 208, 209; **Bud Juneau:** 15, 34, 35, 142, 143, 152, 153, 164; **Milton Gene Kieft:** 30, 31; **Mirco Decet:** 40, 41, 58, 59, 84, 85, 86, 87, 92, 93, 100, 101, 102, 103, 114, 115, 126, 127, 140, 141, 144, 145, 146, 147, 204, 205, 206, 207, 210, 211, 212, 213; **Sam Griffith:** 42, 43, 80, 81, 105, 124, 125, 130, 131, 134, 135, 154, 155; **D. Randy Riggs:** 48, 49; **DarinWalsh, Chevrolet PR:** 50, 51; **Winston Goodfellow:** 54, 55; **Pinifarina:** 76; **Giovanni Perfetti, Ferrari, Modena:** 77; **Thomas Glatch:** 88, 89, 156, 157, 168, 169; **Chuck Johnsen, Mercedes-Benz PR:** 132, 133; **Klaus Parr, Porsche, Germany:** 170, 171, 172, 173, 174, 175, 180, 181, 184, 185; **Jerry Heasley:** 176, 177; **Toyota U.S.A.:** 192, 193, 194, 195, 196, 197.

OWNERS
Special thanks to the owners of the cars featured in this book for their enthusiastic cooperation. They are listed below, along with the page number(s) on which their cars appear:

Steve Levy: Front cover. **Carroll Shelby:** 6; **Collier Auto Museum:** 9; **Tom Barratt:** 10; **Edsel Pfabe:** 11; **Harold Gray:** 11; **Briggs S. Cunningham:** 12, 13; **Colin Fitzgerald:** 14; **Holley Hollenbeck:** 14; **T. Donald Kamm:** 15; **Brooks Stevens Museum:** 15; **Bruce Meyer:** 16, 17; **Dennis Machul:** 26, 27, 65; **Greg Pawluk:** 30, 31; **Graham Love:** 32, 33; **James L. Roman:** 34, 35; **Klaus Lischer:** 36, 37; **Pete Bogard:** 42, 43; **Tom Schay:** 44, 45; **Jack Gersh:** 46, 47; **Joe Heine:** 52, 53; **DeanWilke:** 54, 55; **Mr & Mrs Masson-Styrron:** 58, 59; **Bernie Chase, Symbolic Motor Car Co, La Jolla, CA:** 60, 61, 62, 63, 64, 65, 108, 109; **Dave Cummins:** 66, 67; **Robert J. Pond Automobile Collection:** 68, 69, 70, 71, 74, 75, 78, 79, 128, 129, 150, 151; **Rex Parker Family:** 72, 73; **Steve Levy:** 80, 81; **John Weinberger, Continental Motors, IL:** 82, 83, 116, 117; **P. Doffman:** 84, 85; **Ronald N. Schneider:** 88, 89; **Jack Bart:** 94, 95; **Dennis Gatson:** 96, 97; **Edward Cline:** 98, 99; ; **Yvette Hampton:** 104, 105; **Michael Feldman:** 105; **Jeff Stephan:** 106, 107; **Steve Tillack:** 112, 113; **Harvey Moyses:** 118, 119; **Frank Peiler:** 122, 123; **McLaren Cars Ltd.:** 126, 127; **Don W. Drabik:** 130, 131; **Ben Rose:** 134, 135; **Robert Connole:** 136, 137; **Dennis LeVine:** 138, 139; **Geoff Barron:** 140, 141; **Rear Admiral Thomas J. Patterson:** 142, 143; **Mike Beals, MG Owners Club, England:** 144, 145; **MG PR:** 146, 147; **Bob Sanov, John Willburn:** 148, 149; **Gordon McGregor:** 152, 153; **Johnathan Phillips:** 156, 157; **Tom Mittler:** 157, 162, 163; **C.A. Stoddard:** 158, 159; **Gerry Layer & Richard Simmons:** 160, 161; **Michael F. Hartmann:** 164; **Glenn Sager:** 165; **J.R. Betson, Jr.:** 166, 167; **Barbara Hendrickson;** 168, 169; **Otis Chandler:** 176, 177; **Harvey Caplin, Strasse Automotive:** 178, 179; **Pat Price:** 186, 187; **Thomas Hollfelder:** 188, 189; **George Bearcroft:** 190, 191; **Randy Ressler:** 198, 199; **Mr. Reinhold:** 200, 201; **Adrian Thompson:** 202, 203; **Philippa Newnham:** 204, 205; **Andy Martin:** 206, 207; **Randy & Vicky Huffman:** 208, 209; **Gordon Farqumarson:** 210, 211; **Tim John:** 212, 213.

Thanks to the following for providing vehicles for photography: Andy Boyd, Acura Divison of Honda Motor Corp.; Roger Stowers & Harry Carlton, Aston Martin Lagonda; Bell & Colville, Surrey, England; Valerie Claybush Sherco, BMW of North America; Jaguar Cars Ltd.; Sandro Munari; Lamborghini Automobili SpA; Sam Brown, Group Lotus; Paula Webb, Mclaren Cars Ltd.

This must be reflected in the styling, to please the emotions. And there must be a balance of speed, braking, and turning. It doesn't have to exceeded 160 mph, but without dynamic equilibrium, it's not tangibly a sports car.

To be a *great* sports car demands the strongest presentation of these virtues. For maximum emotional impact, the styling must crystallize the sporting promise. Similarly, performance must make the absolute best use of the technology at hand.

All of which brings us to the contents of this book. Every sports car here defined the breed, and usually improved it. Some advances were small, others groundbreaking. But all set a standard, emotionally and tangibly. Since most manufacturers practice the evolutionary revision of basic designs, we chose the example of each series that was the highest expression of its type. Finally, because postwar models are most relevant today, all the cars profiled here went into production after 1945.

As enthusiasts, we debated the merits of the cars included, and argued over those excluded. We trust you'll do the same, but we also are confident that these 100 automobiles satisfy even the most demanding definition of sports car greatness.

EVOLUTION OF THE SPORTS CAR
1900–1940

In a sense, the earliest automobiles all were sports cars: light, open machines designed to showcase their maker by outperforming rivals. But before long, manufacturers were building cars expressly for sport. Packard pitched its Gray Wolf (above) as a special-order $10,000 production model, though only one was built. In 1904, the 25-hp four-cylinder aluminum-body car set the U.S. speed record, 77.6 mph. The stripped-to-essentials 1903 "Pirate" of Ransom E. Olds (below) was the first car to exceed 60 mph.

In 1900, 40 percent of automobiles were powered by steam, 38 percent had electric motors, and just 22 percent ran on internal combustion. Steam was in fact a popular high-performance fuel at the dawn of the motor age and the brothers Francis and Freelan Stanley were its top proponents (above). Harboring a boiler beneath a trademark coffin-nosed bonnet, their cars easily outaccelerated gasoline machines. In 1906, the Stanleys produced a jaunty little runner called the Gentleman's Speedy Roadster. It could hit 75 mph and was, by any measure, a "sports car." That same year, they built a streamlined steam special with a body that looked like an inverted canoe. With Fred Marriott at the wheel, it hit 127.6 mph on Flordia's Ormond Beach. An internal-combustion car wouldn't run that fast until a Benz driven by Barney Oldfield clocked 131.7 mph in 1910.

These Records Still Stand

Stutz Racing Records are un-equalled after two years of com-petition by the better motor mechanisms of America and Europe, for the same reason that the Sturdy Stutz is giving un-equalled service in owner's hands.

STUTZ MOTOR CAR CO.
Indianapolis, Indiana, U. S. A.

Five Models
$2,000—$2,550
Literature on request

From non-glare lights to tonneau up the Stutz "Bearcat" lives up to its nickname

INDIANAPOLIS
STUTZ
INDIANA, U.S.A.
World's Champion
WORLD'S Speedway Champion
WORLD'S Road Race Champion
World's Long Distance Records 300; 350 - miles
World's Record for Consistency 4 Consecutive 1st & 2nds

STUTZ

Inspired by beach racers, sporty types replaced their car's original heavy coachwork with lighter bodies. Mercer, headquartered in New Jersey, took the cue, built the Type 35 Raceabout (above and top), and the sports car was defined. Built from 1911 to 1915, this triumph of brass, steel, wood, and leather was driven right off the street and into races, including the Indianapolis 500. Its 300-cid four-cylinder engine had 58 hp and could push the 2400-lb car to 80 mph. Two real bucket seats were featured, with a monocle windscreen the only hedge against the elements. The driver sat with right leg outside the car, foot braced on a stirrup, to operate the external accelerator. The Raceabout cost $2150 and about 500 were manufactured

The Indianapolis-built cars of Harry C. Stutz already had a sterling racing record when he introduced the Bearcat in 1914. The initial version was a visual copy of the Raceabout, and though it was larger and less nimble, its overall performance was equally as thrilling. Bearcats were winners on track and road. In 1916, E.G. "Cannonball" Baker drove one coast to coast in 11½ days; nothing but a train had done it faster. The Bearcat was restyled for 1917 (right) and with its 80-hp 360-cid 16-valve four could hit 85 mph. The Bearcat was retired in 1923. The Stutz company by then had new owners, but its sports-car tradition continued in the Black Hawk, which finished second in the 1928 LeMans 24 Hours.

Ferdinand
Porsche's first automobile
was an efficiently designed sports car,
but it wasn't a "Porsche." In 1921, he created for
Austrian Count Sascha Kolowrat a small two-seater with a
1.0-liter ohc four-cylinder. The Sascha (above) did 90 mph and won
the 1100cc class in the '21 Targa Florio. Then as now, the sports-car formula
was open to interpretation. Essex, a low-priced American nameplate, toyed with this
rakish number in 1924 (right). There was no doubt about the magnificent Mercedes-
Benz SSK (below). It meant Super Sport Kurz, or short wheelbase, and represented
unsurpassed workmanship and performance. Road cars built for Grand Prix racing,
they employed a variety of coachwork on a light-alloy chassis. Their 7.1-liter ohc inline-
six rose from 170 hp to a howling 250 when the supercharger was engaged by fully
depressing the accelerator. Top speed was 120 mph. Production spanned 1928 to '34.

Through most of the 1920s, sports cars were playthings of the wealthy. MG changed that with the M-Type Midget (above and right). Built from 1928 to 1932, its cheeky personality, affordability, and happy minimalism drew the blueprint for a legion of British sports cars. Priced low thanks to running gear borrowed from the workaday Morris Minor sedan, the Midget's most advanced feature was an ohc 847cc four-cylinder engine. It had just 20 hp, but the wood-and-fabric boattail body weighed only 2500 lbs, so 60 mph was possible. The car cost the equivalent of $800 and 3235 were manufactured.

Meanwhile, at the other end of the spectrum, Alfa Romeo was producing sports cars to rival Mercedes and Bugatti for engineering excellence and sheer excitement. The 6C1750, introduced in 1929 and built through 1933, is among history's most revered performance automobiles. Designed by Alfa's racing engineer, the great Vittorio Jano, its 1752cc inline-six had dual overhead cams, hemispherical combustion chambers, and aesthetics to rival those of any engine in any era (below). This is the supercharged version, which had 85 hp at 4500 rpm and could push the 2100-lb Alfa to 70 mph in third gear and to 95 in fourth. Several coachbuilders supplied a variety of bodies, from rakish roadsters to closed coupes. All raced, and all won in a day when a thin line separated Grand Prix competition cars from the best roadgoing sports cars. The 6C1750 pictured here is a grand touring roadster built in 1932.

With Mercedes producing powerful heavyweights and Alfa seeking perfectly balanced performance, Ettore Bugatti presented his French-built sports cars as deliberate works of art. Exemplar of this ideal was the Type 55. Just 38 were produced, starting in 1932, and included open and closed coupes, as well as the doorless roadster pictured. The Type 55's two-seat aluminum and steel body rode a 108-inch-wheelbase chassis, which, along with most running gear, came from Bugatti Grand Prix racers. The supercharged 2.3-liter twincam straight-eight is typical of Ettore's engines in its beauty and demand for constant maintenance. It had 135 hp at 5500 rpm and gave the 2016-lb roadster 60 mph in 9.5 seconds and a top speed of 112 mph. Cockpit cables allowed the driver to adjust the shock absorbers, and handling was extraordinary. So was the price: $7525.

Morgan built motorcycle-powered three-wheel cars as cheap British transportation, but also offered real sporting models. The Areo (above) featured a 1096cc ohv JAP vee-twin, could go 70 mph, and was a legitimate sports-car alternative. America's view of 1930's sport motoring ran to size and power. That defined Duesenberg. The Indiana firm built running chassis, which sold for $11,000. With custom bodywork, a Duesie could cost $20,000. This '35 SSJ Roadster had a 125-inch wheelbase instead of the usual 142. The company's renowned supercharged twincam straight-eight had been bored to 450 cid versus 420 and packed 400 hp instead of 320. A twin of one owned by Clark Gable, this Gary Cooper car went 136 mph.

When American GIs stationed in World War II-era England were bitten by the sports-car bug, it was the MG TA (top row) that did much of the nipping. The TA was built from 1936 to '39, weighed 1935 lbs, had a 52-hp 1.3-liter four, and took 23 seconds 0–60 mph. Brits considered it a comedown from previous MGs because it had overhead valves instead of an overhead cam. But Yanks were intoxicated by its lively handling, low mass, cheap price, and cut-down cockpit. The MG introduced them to a new kind of motoring in which the driver was in control rather than just along for the ride. They took this feeling back to the States and helped spark America's infatuation with the genuine sports car.

Nobody was immune from the considerable charms of the SS 100 (right and below). Introduced in 1936, this was the first great sports car from the young British company that was just then changing its name from SS Cars Ltd. to Jaguar. Founder William Lyons was still buying ohv engines and sedan-based running gear from Standard Motor Car Co., but the SS 100 showcased his instincts for style, performance, and value while establishing Jaguar as a marque to be reckoned with.

The SS 100 weighed 2575 lbs and, with the original 104-hp 2.7-liter six, ran 0–60 mph in 12.8 seconds and topped 95 mph. An increase to 3.5 liters for '38 brought 125 hp, 0–60 in under 11 seconds, and a top speed of just over 100 mph. Rear-hinged doors, 18-inch steering wheel, and short-throw four-speed gearbox were part of its character. Best of all, the SS 100 cost less than slower, duller rivals. Just 308 were produced through 1940, but to a generation, this was what sports-car dreams were made of.

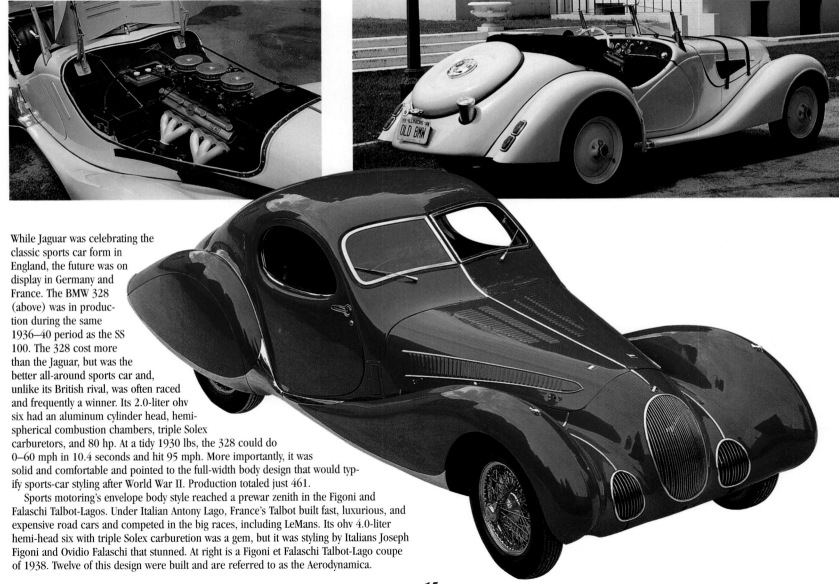

While Jaguar was celebrating the classic sports car form in England, the future was on display in Germany and France. The BMW 328 (above) was in production during the same 1936–40 period as the SS 100. The 328 cost more than the Jaguar, but was the better all-around sports car and, unlike its British rival, was often raced and frequently a winner. Its 2.0-liter ohv six had an aluminum cylinder head, hemispherical combustion chambers, triple Solex carburetors, and 80 hp. At a tidy 1930 lbs, the 328 could do 0–60 mph in 10.4 seconds and hit 95 mph. More importantly, it was solid and comfortable and pointed to the full-width body design that would typify sports-car styling after World War II. Production totaled just 461.

Sports motoring's envelope body style reached a prewar zenith in the Figoni and Falaschi Talbot-Lagos. Under Italian Antony Lago, France's Talbot built fast, luxurious, and expensive road cars and competed in the big races, including LeMans. Its ohv 4.0-liter hemi-head six with triple Solex carburetion was a gem, but it was styling by Italians Joseph Figoni and Ovidio Falaschi that stunned. At right is a Figoni et Falaschi Talbot-Lago coupe of 1938. Twelve of this design were built and are referred to as the Aerodynamica.

AC/SHELBY COBRA 427

*T*exas charm, a promoter's guile, and real talent made Carroll Shelby a world-famous race driver by 1959, when he won LeMans for Aston Martin. A heart condition soon ended his track career, so Shelby turned to his dream of building the world's quickest sports car. The result was a stark terror that ate up the tracks and could bite you on the street.

The Cobra began in 1961 as Carroll's cleverly brokered marriage between the aging-but-light British A.C. Ace roadster and Ford's lively new 260-cid V-8. A stronger 289 quickly followed, giving race-tuned Cobras up to 380 hp and overall 1963 crowns in SCCA A-production and the U.S. Road Racing Championship.

Shelby built 655 small-block Cobras by 1965, when he introduced an even hairier "sport car" (as he termed the breed). Because A.C.'s old transverse-leaf spring suspension was never up to Cobra power, the steel multi-tube frame was widened and strengthened for a modern all-coil setup (still with double wishbones) and for Ford big-block V-8s: either the high-strung racing 427 or the cheaper but equally torquey

428-cid passenger-car unit. The roadster's aluminum body was suitably altered, gaining macho flared fenders stretched over gumball tires.

With nearly 500 hp for just 2500 lbs, the Cobra 427 was "awesome, spellbinding," said *Car and Driver*. "Snapping the throttle open at any speed jams the low seatback into the small of your back. The car lunges, jostles, and belches thunder from the side pipes just below your ear." Although it was surprisingly docile in traffic, *C/D*, like so many, found the car "neither reassuring nor especially comfortable. It rode as if there were cement in the shocks. The steering was indecisive, the handling twitchy and abrupt." Creature comforts? Not here.

Changing times ended this fun in 1968 after only 356 cars, but others soon offered replica 427s ranging in quality from ghastly to grand. A revived A.C. Cars produced its own fine specimen starting in the late '80s. But "Ol' Shel" struck back at his imitators by having 43 brand-new "1965" Cobras built from leftover parts in the mid-'90s. More "snake oil?" Maybe, but also the stuff of living legend and immortal performance.

Among the most brutal sports cars ever was the product of Texan Carroll Shelby's imagination, Ford's NASCAR-tested 427-cid V-8, and a lovely little roadster from A.C. of Britain. The take-no-prisoners AC/Shelby Cobra battled and beat not only Corvette but Ferrari and other purebreds on the world's race tracks. Seasoned competition drivers were hard-pressed to harness its power; on the street, it was a monster of legendary proportion. The car pictured is set up for SCCA racing, so its 427 has a single Holley four-barrel carburetor with a cold air box, a setup rated at 485 hp. Some street versions of the big-block Cobra used a 390-hp 428-cid V-8.

AC/Shelby Cobra 427
1965–1968

Wheelbase, in. 90.0

Weight, lbs. 2530

Price $7500

Engine ohv V-8

Displacement liters/cu. in. 7.0/427

Fuel system 2 x 4 bbl. carburetors

Horsepower @ rpm 425 @ 6500

Torque @ rpm 480 @ 3700

Transmission 4-speed manual

Performance

0–60 mph, sec. 4.5

Top speed, mph 162

ACURA NSX

*T*his marvelous machine demonstrates that in the world of exotic cars, fusing ultra-high performance with impeccable manners may not be such a good thing.

When the NSX—"New Sports car Experimental"—debuted in 1990, eager buyers shelled out nearly twice the $62,000 sticker price. It was the first Japanese automobile to command such a premium, and for good reason.

The NSX can outrun most anything on the road, but it's no high-strung thoroughbred that demands a live-in mechanic to keep in tune and the talent of a Formula 1 champ to enjoy. Instead, it is refined, reliable, and cordial to drivers of modest skill. It's a Honda.

The mid-engine, rear-drive, two-seater showcases the automaker's zeal for efficiency. As the world's first all-aluminum production car, the weight-conscious NSX is light enough to use a compact V-6 engine, which liberates valuable passenger and cargo room. No supercar is more accom-

modating, none is easier to get into and out of, none has simpler controls or better outward visibility. And unlike exotics that eschew modern features in the name of "driver involvement," the NSX and targa-style NSX-T brim with "driver-friendly" technology: dual air bags, anti-lock brakes, traction control, electrically governed power steering and throttle, available automatic transmission with fingertip gear management.

But in avoiding traditional supercar vices, Honda sacrificed an intangible virtue. As *Road & Track* put it, the NSX is "dynamically superb, exceedingly well mannered and civil to a fault . . . the car is a little too ordered and antiseptic, with styling that takes few risks." Indeed, after the initial frenzy, NSX sales declined against idiosyncratic rivals like Porsche and Ferrari.

The open-top NSX-T introduced for 1995 rejuvenated interest and soon accounted for 95 percent of production. But Acura would be thrilled to build 1000 NSXs annually, one-third its original goal. Perfection has its price.

Acura NSX-T
1995–

Wheelbase, in. 99.6

Weight, lbs. 3142

Price $81,000

Engine dohc V-6

Displacement liters/cu. in. 3.0/181

Fuel system Fuel injection

Horsepower @ rpm 270 @ 7100

Torque @ rpm 210 @ 5300

Transmission 5-speed manual

Performance

0–60 mph, sec. 5.3

Top speed, mph 165

Acura's parent company took the typically Honda approach in creating the first Japanese sports exotic. The NSX is efficiently designed and easy to live with. Lightweight all-aluminum construction allows use of a compact V-6 engine for great dynamic balance and a sensibly packaged, no-pain cabin. The Targa version stows its roof panel with no loss of luggage space. Some critics find the NSX uninvolving, but it's a terrific sports car.

ALFA ROMEO GIULIETTA

In naming what would become its most significant car the "Giulietta"—a play on Romeo and Juliet—Alfa Romeo revealed a coy sense of humor. The joke might have been on the Italian automaker had the car itself not been so infatuating.

The Giulietta Spider established Alfa as a builder of attainable sports cars that delighted technically, aesthetically, and dynamically. "A car has no business being so desirable," marveled *Road & Track* after an early fling.

Alfa Romeo came to prominence between the world wars with a series of great and exotic European sporting machines. Its first new postwar design was the 1900 series of 1950. These compact coupes, sedans, and roadsters introduced the marque's wonderful twincam four-cylinder engine and were the first Alfas with unibody construction, affordable prices, and, in a break with racing orientation, the first with lefthand drive.

In 1954, the company stepped into large-scale production with a smaller, sprightlier, and cheaper design than the 1900. Called the 750-Series Giulietta, it consisted of the Sprint, a Bertone-bodied two-door coupe; the Berlina, a factory-styled four-door sedan; and the Spider convertible. The last bowed in 1955 with a lovely Pinin Farina body on a wheelbase 7.1 inches shorter than its stablemates'. All used the 1.3-liter dohc four, but Sprints and Spiders were available in Veloce form with dual sidedraft Webers instead of a single downdraft Solex, 9.1:1 compression instead of 8.5:1, and 10 hp more. The sedan sold best, but the Spider, particularly in Veloce tune, best expressed Alfa's achievement.

It had little low-end torque but would rev to 8000 rpm with an intoxicating snarl. It had a solid rear axle but outhandled rivals with independent rear suspension. It had overengineered drum brakes and enough wheel travel to gobble up bad pavement. There was lots of leg room, rollup windows, an efficient top, even good trunk space. The Giulietta Spider was the first Alfa to make an impact in America, and it engaged enthusiasts everywhere in a long and passionate affair.

Alfa Romeo Giulietta
1955–1959

Wheelbase, in. 86.6

Weight, lbs. 1903

Price $3000

Engine dohc I-4

Displacement liters/cu. in. 1.3/78.7

Fuel system 2 x 2 bbl. carburetors

Horsepower @ rpm 90 @ 7400

Torque @ rpm 87 @ 4500

Transmission 4-speed manual

Performance

0–60 mph, sec. 11.0

Top speed, mph 112

Alfa Romeo forged its reputation for superior road and racing cars between the world wars, but it wasn't until it went mass-market with the charming Giulietta that it reached a wide American audience. Open and closed body styles were offered, the most desirable being the Pinin Farina styled convertible that debuted for 1955. It used a 1.3-liter twincam four that had a modest 80 hp but lots of heart and all the right sounds. Shown is the Veloce version, which added twin Weber carburetors, steel-tube exhaust headers, and other tweaks to produce a welcome 90 hp. Handling was nimble and predictable, and ride quality was outstanding thanks to a well-sorted solid-rear-axle suspension that embarrassed some all-independent setups. From the deftly rendered sheetmetal to the elegant gauges and simple steering wheel, the Giulietta was a jewel.

ALFA ROMEO GIULIA

In 1966, *Road & Track* found it "a contrived design with meaningless styling gimmicks." In 1989, however, the magazine saw "pure beauty and refined aesthetic detail."

Don't fault *Road & Track*; hardly anyone praised Alfa Romeo's follow-up to the beloved Giulietta Spider during its production run. Even the factory reacted by eventually squaring up the distinctive pointed tail. But time has vindicated the Giulia Duetto Spider, the final design credited to Battista Pininfarina himself. Its front and rear symmetry, alluring headlamp covers, and bold bodyside trough is the stuff of automotive art.

Alfa had carried the original Giulietta Spider styling into the succeeding generation of small coupes, sedans, and convertibles. This family debuted for 1962 and was called the Giulia Series, another Romeo and Juliet reference. When finally the next Spider was unveiled in 1966, Alfa fans recognized styling cues from Pininfarina show cars going back a decade. Officially, this was the Giulia Spider 1600, but Alfa held a name-the-car-contest. The winner, one

Guidobaldo Trionfi, riffed on the two-cam, two-seat, two-carburetor motif and came up with Duetto.

It was more refined than the Giulietta Spider, heavier and with a longer wheelbase. It retained a solid rear axle but got four-wheel disc brakes. Underhood was the 1.6-liter four that bowed in the Giulia but now with standard twin Webers and a five-speed gearbox.

Emissions rules kept Alfa from the U.S. market in 1968, but the roundtail roadster returned for '69 with a fuel-injected 1977cc enlargement of the 1600. Alfa tabbed this the 1750, recalling its famous prewar cars. Purists insist the 1750 is not a true Duetto; more-generous Alfisti say the tapered tail qualifies it as one. These cars had 132 hp, did 0–60 in 9.9 seconds, and hit 114 mph. U.S. smog laws shut out the '70 Spider, and when it returned for '71, it had a squared rump and no claim to the Duetto name. The core of Pininfarina's brilliant original design survived, however, until 1993, when Alfa at last retired the Spider.

Alfa Romeo Giulia
1966–1970

Wheelbase, in. 88.6

Weight, lbs. 2195

Price $4050

Engine dohc I-4

Displacement liters/cu. in. 1.6/95.6

Fuel system 2 x 2 bbl. carburetors

Horsepower @ rpm 125 @ 6000

Torque @ rpm 115 @ 2800

Transmission 5-speed manual

Performance

0–60 mph, sec. 11.3

Top speed, mph 113

Alfa Romeo's follow-up to the beloved Giulietta was the controversially styled Duetto Spider. When it bowed for 1966, critics dismissed its tapered nose and tail and deep bodyside trough as trifles. But over time, these elements came to identify a classic design from the house of Pininfarina. The car itself was more refined than the Giulietta Spider and offered such upgrades as a five-speed gearbox and four-wheel disc brakes. Acceleration was never a strong suit and the handling, laudable in the '60s, was surpassed by front-drive hatchbacks in the 1970s. Still, there was enough character here to sustain the Spider's basic design all the way to 1993.

ALLARD J2X

Sydney Herbert Allard was a Brit with the soul of a California hot rodder, and the charming brutes he built won fans' hearts in the golden days of American sports-car racing. Powered by bellowing Detroit V-8s, his cycle-fender specials were the epitome of low-dollar motorsports in the early 1950s—backyard brawlers taking on costly Ferraris.

Allard's hot-rodding roots were in 1930s England, where he won races and rallies in homebuilt jalopies with hopped-up flathead Ford V-8s. After the war, he went into small-scale production of Ford-powered sports coupes and convertibles, even driving one to victory in the 1952 Monte Carlo Rally. Most successful were his sports-racers, starting with the Mercury V-8-powered J1 roadster of 1947. This was succeeded by the J2: Allard built 90 of these and drove one to third place overall in the 1950 24 Hours of LeMans. In 1952, came the J2X, which earned its stripes on America's colorful old road courses and airfield tracks.

Like the J2, it was a narrow two-seater with cycle fenders, but its frame was extended six inches—hence the "X"—to the benefit of leg room and handling. Most used modern 5.4-liter V-8s from Chrysler or Cadillac and had up to 235 hp. In front was a Ford beam axle cut and pivoted in the middle to create a crude semi-independent suspension that generated some wild front camber angles. In addition, the car could appear to "crab" because the rear track was four inches narrower than the front.

At speed, a J2X was a spectacular handful: tail hunkered down from the V-8's torque, nose elevated, tires akimbo. "The sight of an Allard under full cornering load made strong men bite through their pipe stems and children cry for their mothers," wrote Allan Girdler in his book *American Road Race Specials 1934–70.*

Still, from Watkins Glen to Pebble Beach they won, finally succumbing in 1954 to more sophisticated factory machines. The tiny Allard Motor Company ceased production in 1959, but the automobiles it built were the stuff of sports-car legend.

Allard J2X
1952–1954

Wheelbase, in. 100.0

Weight, lbs. 2500

Price NA

Engine dohc ohv V-8

Displacement liters/cu. in. 5.4/331

Fuel system 4 x 1 bbl. carburetors

Horsepower @ rpm 230 @ 4400

Torque @ rpm 330 @ 2700

Transmission 3-speed manual

Performance

0–60 mph, sec. 8.0

Top speed, mph 125

Classic English cycle-fender styling and serious Detroit power—in this case a quad-carb Cadillac V-8—gave the J2X loads of character. Harrowing to drive, these British/Yankee backyard specials used stout construction and lots of torque to overcome a crude suspension and beat fancy factory machines in the early days of American sports-car racing.

ASTON MARTIN DB4GT

Aston Martin peaked in the public eye when its DB5 coupe stole the show in 1964's *Goldfinger.* In reality, James Bond's machine-gunning wonder had an even more impressive antecedent, one famous for delivering blazing speed, not hot lead.

This quintessential British maker of elegant, low-volume performance cars was founded in 1913 by Singer dealers Lionel Martin and Robert Bumford. Racers at heart, they drew on the Aston Hillclimb for part of the name, and their early cars dominated English trials and speed events. But competition success didn't spell financial security, and in 1947, British industrialist David Brown bought the company. His DB1 and DB2 were prelude to the DB4 of 1958, the first truly modern Aston.

Its body, by Touring of Milan, used aluminum panels over a tubular lattice—Touring's patented "super light" or *Superleggera* construction. Although the DB4 still weighed nearly 3000 lbs, it could do 141 mph. When the racing DBR1 won the LeMans 24 Hours outright in 1959 and helped Brown snare the world sports-car championship,

buyers begged for faster Astons. In 1959, he gave them the DB4GT.

This was basically a DB4 coupe, but wheelbase was cut five inches, eliminating the small rear seats and helping shed nearly 200 lbs. Under the bonnet was a new version of the DB4's glorious all-alloy 3.7-liter inline-six with high-lift cams, 9.0:1 compression (versus 8.25:1), three Webers instead of two SUs, and 62 hp more. Aston had a world-class performer. Nothing *Car and Driver* tested in 1961 or '62 was quicker 0–60 mph than the DB4GT. It cost about $2000 more than the regular DB4 and, in speed and style, approached the $20,000 Ferrari 250 GTO, which was not nearly as civilized.

Race-prepped DB4GTs did well on longer circuits, but the car was too heavy to win consistently. A run of 19 lighter Zagato-bodied DB4GTs were built in 1960, but there was no money to challenge the serious factory teams. Aston refocused on grand-touring luxury and produced the famous DB5, a sports car more at home on the silver screen than at Silverstone.

Aston Martin DB4GT
1959–1963

Wheelbase, in. 93.0

Weight, lbs. 2705

Price $12,500

Engine dohc I-6

Displacement liters/cu. in. 3.7/224

Fuel system 3 x 2 bbl. carburetors

Horsepower @ rpm
302 @ 6000

Torque @ rpm 240 @ 2800

Transmission 4-speed manual

Performance

0–60 mph, sec. 6.4

Top speed, mph 142

Most Americans link Aston Martin with James Bond's DB5 spy car, but the marque has a much richer history. Its best all-around sports car built in any numbers was the DB4GT. Italy's Touring did the styling and put aluminum body panels over a tubular lattice in its patented "super light" or Superleggera construction. Aston's twincam six got 302 hp from 224 cubic inches for rousing performance. The well-appointed interior testifies to the DB4GT's road-car origins, while the racing livery and roll bar reveal this example as one that also competed. Just 74 DB4GTs were were built. Another 19 had more exotic bodies by Zagato.

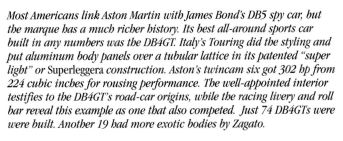

ASTON MARTIN DB7

*D*ynamically, the DB7 is as good as it needs to be, and at $125,000 ($135,000 for the convertible), it needs to be plenty good. But the obligation of a car like this is to provide its owner that which isn't measured by stopwatch or skidpad.

Introduced in Europe in 1995 and in America in '96, the DB7 was the first Aston Martin developed under Ford Motor Company, which took control of Aston in 1987. Ford also owns Jaguar, and the DB7 shares with the new Jaguar XK8 a Jaguar XJS central floorpan; its engine block is also of Jaguar origin. Ford money helped develop, test, and certify both cars, but the DB7 was designed by Aston to be an Aston—to carry on its defining DB series, in fact.

Thus it has a refined dohc inline-six enhanced by an Eaton supercharger. Acceleration is best described as rapid; the DB7 is too heavy to be quick. It feels sportiest with the Getrag five-speed, though virtually all U.S. cars get a General Motors four-speed automatic. Ride is composed on every surface, braking is strong and, despite uninvolved

steering, the car is balanced, sticky, and predictable in turns. This is a sporting machine that makes few demands on its driver, but it is not the DB7's performance that will compel a purchase. Neither will the 2+2 cabin, which relies on Connolly hides and gleaming walnut to divert attention from generic switchgear.

A stronger lure is the voluptuous body. The mix of steel and composite panels is unique to the DB7, despite a visual similarity to the XK8. Styled by Aston's Ian Callum, formerly of Ford's Ghia studio, the shape is contemporary but respects the magnificent DB4, DB5, and DB6, especially in the charismatic grille opening.

Combine that look with exclusivity—production of just 650 per year, a scant 200 for America—and the DB7's nature is revealed. The new sports car from Aston Martin represents discriminating taste, a certain breeding. It is not Italian, and it certainly is not German. In a realm where price is irrelevant, a car must make its owner *feel special.* The DB7 does.

Aston Martin DB7
1995–

Wheelbase, in. 102.0

Weight, lbs. 3803

Price $125,000

Engine Supercharged dohc I-6

Displacement liters/cu. in. 3.2/224

Fuel system Fuel injection

Horsepower @ rpm 335 @ 5750

Torque @ rpm 361 @ 3000

Transmission 5-speed manual

Performance

0–60 mph, sec. 5.5

Top speed, mph 165

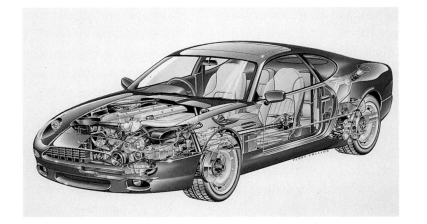

Even at an annual production of just 670, the DB7 qualifies as the highest-volume Aston Martin ever. It appeals to those with a refined sense of sport-motoring history and the ability to pay more than $125,000 to indulge it. What they'll get is an equally refined GT coupe or Volante convertible with a well-toned supercharged six, athletic suspension, patrician interior, and sublime styling. The DB7's appearance is similar to that of the new Jaguar XK8, but the cars differ greatly in detail and attitude.

AUSTIN-HEALEY 100

*S*edan-based sports cars existed long before Donald Healey, but he built some of the best. Like many of our 100 Greatest, his Austin-Healey exceeded the sum of its parts.

Healey was an ace rally driver known throughout Europe and his native England in the 1920s, then was technical chief at Triumph. He long wanted to build his own car but had little money for tooling. By 1946, however, he'd designed a rugged chassis, found body suppliers, and secured powerteams, mainly from Riley. With that, his small Warwickshire shop turned out handfuls of genuine 100-mph sports cars through 1954, including the racy, cycle-fendered Silverstone roadster and the Anglo-American Nash-Healey.

Trouble was, these cars were costly to build and buy, and Healey wanted bigger sales and profits. Accordingly, he designed for the 1952 London Motor Show a new two-seater based on the cheap, workaday Austin 90 sedan. With sleek envelope body styling by Donald's friend Gerry Coker, the "Healey 100" prototype impressed Leonard Lord, managing director

of Austin's parent, the British Motor Corporation. Lord bought the design on the spot, giving Austin its first true sports car and Healey a windfall.

Named for its top speed, the Austin-Healey 100 was modern for its day, with a unit body/chassis and coil-spring independent front suspension. Austin's big 90-hp 2.7-liter four-cylinder engine was old but trusty, as the cars soon proved by winning races and rallies around the globe. In 1954, Healey's shops (not BMC) delivered 55 competition versions, the 100S ("Sebring") with aluminum bodywork instead of steel and 132 hp. A bit later came the 100M ("modified"), a snazzy two-tone job with 110 hp and numerous race-oriented tweaks. Healey built 1159 of those.

But the basic 100 was a far greater success. Austin sold more than 10,000 of the 1953–55 "BN1" and nearly 4000 of the improved 1955–56 "BN2" models with four-speed (instead of three-speed) gearbox. Such volume was a dream-come-true for Healey and Austin, but it was not hard to fathom. The A-H was more modern than an MG, faster than a Triumph TR, and far more affordable than a Jaguar XK.

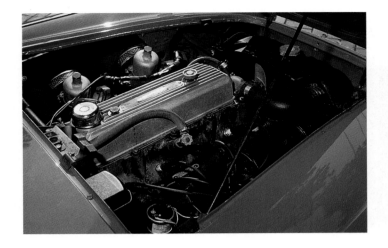

***Austin-Healey 100
1953–1956***

Wheelbase, in. 90.0

Weight, lbs. 2175

Price $2100

Engine ohv I-4

Displacement liters/cu. in. 2.7/162

Fuel system 2 x 1 bbl. carburetors

Horsepower @ rpm 90 @ 4000

Torque @ rpm 144 @ 4000

Transmission 3-speed manual

Performance

0–60 mph, sec. 10.3

Top speed, mph 103

Sturdy, handsome, and a good performer for its day, the Autsin-Healey 100 blended the sports-car acumen of Donald Healey with the production capacity and trusty engine of the British Motor Corporation's Austin division. The example pictured is a first series A-H 100, known as the BN1. Standard features included a racy lay-back windshield. This car quickly established a fine reputation, especially in the United States, where enthusiasts recognized it as far more modern than the contemporary MG TF. In fact, most of the more than 14,000 BN1s and BN2s built were sold in America.

AUSTIN-HEALEY 3000

*T*here wasn't much wrong with the Austin-Healey 100 that a bigger engine couldn't fix, which is why the original "100/4" (a retrospective title) became the 100 Six in late 1956. Alas, this longer, heavier, cushier car—complete with tiny "+2" rear seats—was less responsive and not much faster despite its new six-cylinder engine and extra 12 hp. Within a year came a new cylinder head for five more hp and more torque. Top speed rose 8 mph to 111, 0–60-mph sprints fell nearly two seconds to 11.2. A two-seater returned by 1958 on the same 92-inch wheelbase.

That same year, British Motor Corporation introduced the small and cheeky Sprite for buyers on a budget and the "Big Healey" moved upmarket. The revised 3000 of 1959 was named for an engine enlarged to nearly 3.0 liters and 124 hp. Also new were front disc brakes (drums continued aft), plus vertical bars on the hood scoop and an oval grille. Performance improved again, now nearly 115 mph flat-out and just over 11 seconds 0–60. Two years later, BMC unveiled the 3000 Mark II, which was little faster despite another eight hp from new triple carburetion. A better-shifting

gearbox was a welcome running change before the roadster was thoroughly updated to become the Mark II Convertible, with integral top, curved windshield, and, to the dismay of some, door ventwings and rollup windows. Twin carbs returned but power was unchanged. Not for long.

Spring 1964 ushered in the 3000 Mark III with 148 hp, plus center console and a restyled wood-veneered dash. A "Phase II" model bowed later that year with longer suspension travel and better rear-axle location. Now the Mark III was not only the best-handling Big Healey but the fastest. It was also the most popular of this breed with 17,704 sold (versus 25,213 total earlier models). But it couldn't last. The basic design was too old to justify the expense of meeting new U.S. safety and emissions rules, so the Big Healey was left to die after 1967. Donald Healey and his son Geoff moved on to other things, but for many, the 3000 will always be their best work. It was, as motoring journalist Cyril Posthumus once wrote, "incredibly rough and solid, yet handsome and amazingly cheap. In short, a lovable bastard."

Austin-Healey 3000 Mark III
1964–1967

Wheelbase, in. 92.0

Weight, lbs. 2550

Price $3500

Engine ohv I-6

Displacement liters/cu. in. 2.9/177

Fuel system 2 x 1 bbl. carburetors

Horsepower @ rpm 148 @ 5250

Torque @ rpm 165 @ 3500

Transmission 4-speed manual

Performance

0–60 mph, sec. 9.8

Top speed, mph 121

British Motor Corporation updated its powertrains with a 2.6-liter six in 1956, and the new engine was a natural for the Austin-Healey. Thus, the 100/4 became the 100 Six. Enlarged to 2.9 liters, the six formed the basis for a slightly revised A-H sports car released in 1959 and called the 3000. The 3000's final and best iteration bowed in 1964 as the Mark III. As did all the Big Healeys, the Mark III boasted rugged construction, a heavy but reliable engine, smooth styling, and a hairy-chested, rumbly personality. Snug and well equipped, it was equally comfortable open and closed. By the mid-1960s, however, the 3000 was looking old-fashioned. BMC decided that modifying the car for new U.S. safety and emission regulations wasn't worth the money and the Big Healy was consigned to history after 1967. The steering wheel on the example pictured is an aftermarket piece.

BMW 507

*G*iven its reputation for stylish, carefully engineered driving machines, it's difficult to imagine BMW as a purveyor of automotive oddities. But that was the case after World War II, and it took a sports car to straighten things out.

Bavarian Motor Works, builder of fine motorcycles and exciting roadsters in the 1920s and '30s, was a postwar disaster. Those of its facilities not stranded behind the Iron Curtain lay devastated by Allied bombs. When BMW limped back to production in 1951, it was with a big, ugly sedan derided as the "Baroque Angel." And its tiny 1955 Isetta "egg car"—that of the single front door—defined bizarre. Meanwhile, in America, import-car baron Max Hoffman saw a market for a European sports car to fill the mid-price gap between MG and Mercedes-Benz. Hoffman approached BMW with his proposal, and the German company responded with the 507.

It employed the Baroque Angel's sound chassis design, steering, and suspension, but used a new substructure on a 16-inch shorter wheelbase. The aluminum bodywork was by freelance designer Count Albrecht Goertz, who went on to style the Datsun 240Z. With or without the optional lift-off steel hardtop, the fluid 507 was the visual knockout BMW desperately needed.

Under the long hood was an enlarged version of the sedan's V-8. It had 150 hp and, with the standard 3.70:1 axle, could deliver 120 mph; 140 was possible with the optional 3.42:1 ratio and 160-hp tuning. "When driven modestly, the V-8 engine is smooth, quiet and docile," reported *Road & Track*. "Yet, given full throttle through the gears, the kitten becomes a tiger and really leaps."

Torsion bars and a live rear axle provided acceptable handling, but the 507 wasn't nimble, being heavier than its lean looks implied. And not until front disc brakes replaced drums late in production did stopping power match speed potential. The 507 was highly desirable, however, and, as it turned out, highly exclusive. Hoffman envisioned it selling for $5000, but when the virtually hand-built sports car went on sale, the U.S. price was an astronomical $9000. Few were ordered, but the 507 restored BMW to a performance footing that defines the company today.

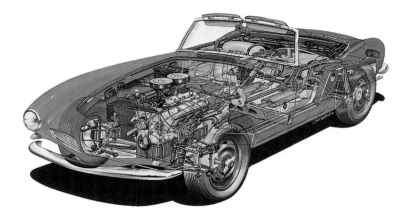

BMW 507
1956–1959

Wheelbase, in. 97.6

Weight, lbs. 2935

Price $9000

Engine ohv V-8

Displacement liters/cu. in. 3.2/370

Fuel system 2 x 2 bbl. carburetors

Horsepower @ rpm 150 @ 5000

Torque @ rpm 173 @ 5200

Transmission 4-speed manual

Performance

0–60 mph, sec. 8.8

Top speed, mph 124

It took BMW until 1956 to retake the sports-car heights it had reached with the prewar 328. Its comeback was the virile 507, a two-seater based on the company's beefy sedan chassis. Knockout aluminum bodywork was styled by German Albrecht Goertz. The overhead valve V-8 wasn't high-tech, but was strong and well-mannered. Same for the live-rear-axle suspension. The 507 was a critical success, but ended up costing $9000 and just 253 were built. Still, it said BMW was back.

BMW M1

*I*t was fast, agile, and dramatic, but its true significance was as the world's first untemperamental supercar. This civility was all the more remarkable because the M1 began life as a genuine racing machine.

The M1—"mid-engine car, first type"— was conceived in 1975 as BMW's Porsche fighter in the prestigious World Championship of Makes. Since BMW had to build 400 production examples to qualify the M1 for racing, it was no surprise that the roadgoing version was a supremely competent high-performance car. Its structure was engineered to handle racing engines of as much as 850 hp, its suspension, steering, and braking systems designed to spar with Porsche 935s. Unexpected was the M1's proficiency as an everyday transportation device.

"Out of some rare sense of automotive honor, its builders took enormous care to make a real car out of a concept so many others have treated with disdainful surreality," wrote Pete Lyons in *Car and Driver*. The M1 was roomy, comfortable, and constructed with care. It had good outward visibility and 6.2 cubic feet of insulated luggage space. The engine was tractable and didn't overheat. All in all, rival exotics were spoiled brats by comparison. But nothing as good as the M1 comes easily.

Giorgetto Giugiaro's Ital Design had been hired to style the fiberglass body and Lamborghini to build the car. BMW's main contribution was the engine: a much-modified 24-valve version of its proven inline-six. Disorganized Lamborghini could deliver only about 12 M1s before BMW was forced to farm out construction to two other Italian firms and turn over final assembly to a German coachbuilder.

By the time full-scale production began in 1979, the M1's race series was in decline and the roughly two-dozen competition versions never really got a chance to show their stuff. BMW let the car die, its true potential unrealized. "It could have redefined exotic sports cars more as polished driving instruments, less as shiny fashion accessories," lamented Lyons. "The M1 deserved to found a dynasty."

BMW M1
1978–1981

Wheelbase, in. 100.8

Weight, lbs. 3325

Price $87,000

Engine dohc I-6

Displacement liters/cu. in. 3.5/210

Fuel system Fuel injection

Horsepower @ rpm 277 @ 7400

Torque @ rpm 242 @ 5000

Transmission 5-speed manual

Performance

0–60 mph, sec. 5.5

Top speed, mph 162

BMW's first and only mid-engine production car was conceived as a racing machine, but the M1 never really got a chance to compete because of assembly delays and rules changes. Instead, it became a groundbreaking road car, the first to combine real supercar credentials with civilized manners. Its 3.5-liter inline-six was strong yet tractable and didn't bake luggage thanks to an insulated cargo-bay. The roomy cabin featured a friendly driving position and fine outward visibility. BMW built just 450 M1s, leaving its promise unfulfilled.

BMW Z3

*P*ower-hungry types said they'd wait for the six-cylinder version. Fashion hounds criticized the front-end styling. No one warmed to the meek exhaust note. But the Z3 goes its own way. Being a BMW, there's a certain maturity about it, and for those who can forgive the modest engine output and stir its shifter, the rewards are many.

On sale in spring 1996, the Z3 beat Mercedes-Benz's SLK and Porsche's Boxster to market in the European roadster renaissance of the mid-1990s. Juiced by an overhyped cameo in the James Bond flick *GoldenEye*, demand for the Z3 deluged BMW's just-opened South Carolina factory, which was the car's sole worldwide source.

Part of the allure was the Z3's overtly sporty long-hood, short-deck proportions, though some observers found the globular nose a mismatch for the rest of the body. BMW said the decorative front-fender vents "can be interpreted as a small stylistic tribute to the BMW 507 roadster."

Comparisons with the Mazda Miata were natural and showed the BMW to be seven inches longer in wheelbase, three inches longer overall, and nearly 400 lbs heavier. Both cars have a manual soft top with a plastic rear window, though the Z3 easily has more passenger and cargo room.

To control costs, BMW reused the semitrailing-arm rear suspension from an earlier-generation 3-Series sedan, a design Z3 press materials defend as "appealing uncomplicated." It works, though, and except for occasionally jitterbugging its tail in fast, bumpy turns, the Z3 is composed, balanced, and agile. A bonus is a supple ride and nearly flex-free construction deserving of the BMW rondel.

Less worthy, at least in specification, is the 1.9-liter four-cylinder engine. It has little low-end punch and never seems really to stir the soul. But its smoothness invites running near the 6400-rpm redline. There, the car feels alert and modern drivers can experience the sporting flavor of a bygone era.

For while the four-cylinder Z3 is thoroughly modern in its dual air bags, anti-lock brakes, and optional traction control, it's a throwback to the days when high speeds didn't come so easily, when one could exercise a sports car to its full potential without risking limb or license. That's rewarding by any measure.

BMW Z3
1996–

Wheelbase, in. 96.3

Weight, lbs. 2746

Price $29,320

Engine dohc I-4

Displacement liters/cu. in. 1.9/116

Fuel system Fuel injection

Horsepower @ rpm 138 @ 6000

Torque @ rpm 133 @ 4300

Transmission 5-speed manual

Performance

0–60 mph, sec. 8.1

Top speed, mph 115

Inspired in part by the success of the Mazda Miata, European automakers staged a roadster revival in the mid-1990s. First to market was the BMW Z3. With its naturally aspirated four-cylinder engine, manual-gearbox, and do-it-yourself folding top, it was more conventional than the Mercedes-Benz SLK or Porsche Boxster. Some were disappointed with the 138-hp Z3's relatively ordinary acceleration and sedan exhaust note. But responsive handling, fine ride, and pleasant accommodations were not to be taken lightly. A far-more-powerful six-cylinder version waited in the wings, but the four-cylinder Z3 offered modern drivers a taste of the days when going fast in a sports car required some skill.

BUGATTI EB 110S

*E*ttore Bugatti was an Italian who settled in France to breed *pur sang* horses—and automobiles. He spent 30 of his 66 years on just 7800 cars. Most were exquisitely engineered racers and sports tourers renowned for handling, performance, even mechanical beauty. Sadly, there was no one to carry on after *Le Patron*'s passing in 1947, and his company died nine years later. But his cars were immortal, and many enthusiasts hoped for the marque's eventual return.

It came in late 1987, with word that a new Bugatti Automobili was being formed in Modena, Italy, to produce a mid-engine supercar rivaling anything from neighboring Ferrari. The chief instigators were two Lamborghini luminaries, engineer Paolo Stanzani and designer Marcello Gandini. But the real power was Romano Artioli, a rich car dealer with an ego worthy of *Le Patron*. Stanzani ran afoul of it in 1990, and was fired by Artioli after attempting a company takeover. Gandini soon departed, too.

This left Artioli to shepherd completion of the EB110 GT, belatedly unveiled in September 1991 to honor Ettore's 110th birthday. Every

inch a modern supercar, it was a coupe with carbon-fiber construction, all-wheel drive, six-speed gearbox, and a new 3.5-liter alloy V-12 boasting 60 valves and four turbochargers. Claimed horsepower was 550, and in 1992 came a bespoiled 110S (a.k.a. Sport Stradale) with an incredible 620. Astounding performance seemed guaranteed, and the legendary Phil Hill confirmed it by taking an S to 213.1 mph for a January 1995 *Road & Track* feature. "You can cruise at over 200 mph like you're on an ordinary road," Hill enthused. "The steering is lovely and the gearbox delightful. It's just an outstanding car!"

But the 110 was already doomed by Artioli, who set up an engineering consultancy, a Bugatti museum, and a merchandising division before selling many cars. And sales were almost impossible with six-figure prices and a tightening world economy. A desperate Artioli bought Lotus of England in August '93, but that only lost more money. Bugatti was bankrupt by late 1995, thus squandering an exciting sports car and the promising rebirth of a hallowed marque.

Bugatti EB 110S
1992–1995

Wheelbase, in. 100.4

Weight, lbs. 3875

Price $350,000

Engine Quad turbo dohc V-12

Displacement liters/cu. in. 3.5/214

Fuel system Fuel injection

Horsepower @ rpm 620 @ 8250

Torque @ rpm 462 @ 3750

Transmission 6-speed manual

Performance

0–60 mph, sec. 3.2

Top speed, mph 220

The name once identified with the prewar world's most cultured sports cars returned in the 1990s on a state-of-the-art supercar. With four turbos, all-wheel drive, carbon-fiber materials, and 620 hp, the EB 110S was a 200-mph tour de force. But its backers were inept and a proud name went down with them.

CHEVROLET CORVETTE

"America's Sensational Sports Car!" screamed the very first Corvette advertisement in May 1953. The claim was a little premature. Corvette looked like a sports car but was saddled with Chevy's 150-hp Blue Flame inline-six and slushy Powerglide two-speed automatic. The fiberglass roadster went 0–60 in 11 seconds and hit 105 mph—OK for the day—but not enough to overcome its poor handling and high price. Chevrolet hoped to sell 20,000 for 1954, the car's first full year. It built just 3640.

Chevy considered dropping the Corvette, but suddenly needed it to counter Ford's new Thunderbird. Luckily, the 265-cid Turbo-Fire V-8 was ready for '55, and the 195-hp 'Vette could do 0–60 in 8.5 seconds and top 115 mph, though there was no manual gearbox until late in the year. Production dipped to 647, just four percent of T-Bird sales. But German-trained engineer Zora Arkus-Duntov had arrived and a transformation was afoot. Into the redesigned '56 went a revamped 265 with a hot Duntov cam and up to 240 hp. Zero–60 fell to 7.5 seconds and pro-

duction recovered to 3467. But it was the '57 Corvette that finally lived up to the boast of that original ad.

The 265 became a 283, creating Chevy's storied small-block V-8. It had up to 270 hp with dual quads and reached the magical one horsepower per cubic inch when equipped with GM's newly developed "Ramjet" fuel injection. Just as significant was replacement of the three-speed manual with a four-speed. Armed with the $725 "heavy-duty racing suspension" package (including quick-ratio steering and ceramic-metallic brake linings with finned drums), 283-hp four-speed 'Vettes were production-class winners. The high point was Sebring, where Corvettes were 1–2 in the GT class and 12th and 15th overall.

"Before Sebring," said one European writer, "the Corvette was regarded as a plastic toy. After Sebring, even the most biased were forced to admit that the Americans had one of the world's finest sports cars—as capable on the track as it was on the road. Those who drove and understood the Corvette could not help but reach that conclusion."

**Chevrolet Corvette
1955–1962**

Wheelbase, in. 102.0

Weight, lbs. 3180

Price $4098

Engine ohv V-8

Displacement liters/cu. in. 4.6/283

Fuel system Fuel injection

Horsepower @ rpm 283 @ 6200

Torque @ rpm 290 @ 4400

Transmission 4-speed manual

Performance

0–60 mph, sec. 5.7

Top speed, mph 132

Saddled with an uninspired six-cylinder engine and poor handling, the original Corvette wasn't much of a sports car. By 1955, it had a V-8 and a new patron saint, German-trained engineer Zora Arkus-Duntov. His intensity paid off for '57, when the 'Vette got Chevy's new 283-cid V-8. With GM's new fuel-injection system, the storied small-block made one horsepower per cubic inch and put Corvette on the performance-car map. Equipped with the optional heavy-duty racing suspension, handling was world-class, too. Of 6339 'Vettes built for '57, this is one of 240 with the fuel-injected engine.

CHEVROLET CORVETTE STING RAY

*E*ngineer Zora Arkus-Duntov opposed it. Hampered outward vision, he said. Chief designer William Mitchell supported it. Vital to the car's character, he said. "If you take that off," huffed Mitchell, "you might as well forget the whole thing." They both were right.

Divided by a thick vertical bar, the split rear window of the 1963 Corvette coupe was the car's defining stylistic element—and it so interfered with rear visibility that it was replaced by a one-piece pane for '64. The '63's significance goes beyond that split window, of course: The only all-new Corvette between the 1953 Motorama original and the 1984 model, it launched the car's classic period.

Both its Sting Ray name and general shape came from Mitchell's 1950s Stingray racer. Nothing was shared with the '62 model except steering, front suspension, and four 327-cid V-8s. The 327 had replaced the 283 for '62, and the hottest fuel-injected version now made 360 hp.

Fiberglass returned for the body of the convertible and the dramatic

new coupe. The tail design was first seen on the '61 'Vette but now was mirrored by a tapered prow that hid the headlamps in rotating housings. Wheelbase was four inches shorter than before, and a ladder-type frame replaced the heavy X-member chassis. Weight was down, and for the first time in a front-engine American production car, more than half of it was on the rear wheels. Handling was further enhanced by independent rear suspension, another breakthrough in a modern U.S. production car. With new options—leather, power steering and brakes, even air conditioning—a 'Vette could be a posh GT, all-out screamer, or both.

Over the next four years, the Sting Ray got cleaner styling, more power, and greater mechanical sophistication. The fuelie small-block delivered up to 395 hp for '64, while '65 brought optional four-wheel discs and Corvette's first big-block V-8, the 425-hp 396-cid "Mark IV." The next year saw a bored-out 427. On racetracks, Sting Rays were frustrated by Carroll Shelby's stark Cobras. But on the road, it took an extravagantly priced imported exotic to catch America's sports car.

Chevrolet Corvette Sting Ray 1963–1967

Wheelbase, in. 98.0

Weight, lbs. 3150

Price $5300

Engine ohv V-8

Displacement liters/cu. in. 5.4/327

Fuel system Fuel injection

Horsepower @ rpm 360 @ 6000

Torque @ rpm 352 @ 4000

Transmission 4-speed manual

Performance

0–60 mph, sec. 5.8

Top speed, mph 135

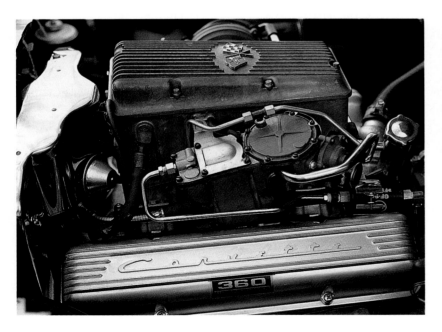

For 1963, Corvette got its first redesign since being introduced a decade earlier and celebrated with a coupe body style. The spine of fiberglass intersecting the backlight was present only on the '63 and gave the closed car its now-renowned nickname—the split-window coupe. Hidden headlamps were another new trademark, but they lasted through the end of the second generation in 1967. The '63 'Vette was the first modern American production car with independent rear suspension and the first with more than half its weight over the rear tires. Its fuel-injected 327 had 360 hp, and would be followed by big-block stormers that had even more power but less friendly handling.

CHEVROLET CORVETTE 427 STINGRAY

Chevy's third-generation Corvette began life as one of the world's fiercest sports cars. It ended life something less, but it was so right for the times that its popularity grew as its performance declined.

Chassis and engines were essentially carryovers from the 1963–67 series and mated with a new seven-inch-longer body inspired by the '65 Mako Shark II show car. Convertible and coupe returned, the latter with removable "T-tops." All-disc brakes were made standard, and GM's three-speed Turbo Hydra-Matic replaced the archaic two-speed Powerglide automatic. Actually, the '68 Corvette would've bowed for 1967 had Zora Arkus-Duntov not delayed it to work out some kinks. Still, it had poor workmanship and weak engine cooling, a cramped interior, and gimmicks such as a troublesome pop-up windshield-wiper panel. But this was the only American automobile designed for serious handling and ruthless acceleration. Whether it was a "sports car" was irrelevant.

The Shark generation boasted some impressive small-block V-8s—the 1970 350-cid LT1 had 370 hp—but Corvette was feared for its big-

blocks. The largest was a 454 cid (1970 to '74), but the most exciting were the 427s of '68 and '69. With more horsepower than cubic inches, these remarkably free-revving V-8s demonstrated what Detroit could do with a pushrod design, and their power sent road testers to the thesaurus. After a blast in a tri-carb '69 coupe, *Car and Driver* admitted to "more open combat with similes and metaphors . . . in an attempt to describe the exact sensation in the region of the fourth pelvic vertebrae when the throttle is punched on a 427-cid 435-horsepower Stingray . . ."

Corvette performance would soon dial back to meet new laws, insurance pressures, and public expectations. Big-blocks and the LT1 disappeared after '74, and by '82 there was no manual gearbox. But annual production in most of the Shark years was well over 40,000, and Chevy sold nearly 54,000 '79s—astonishing numbers for a high-performance two-seater. What Corvette couldn't overtake on the road, it trounced in the showroom.

Chevrolet Corvette 427 Stingray 1968–1969

Wheelbase, in. 98.0

Weight, lbs. 3450

Price $6500

Engine ohv V-8

Displacement liters/cu. in. 7.0/427

Fuel system 3 x 2 bbl. carburetors

Horsepower @ rpm 435 @ 5800

Torque @ rpm 460 @ 4000

Transmission 4-speed manual

Performance

0–60 mph, sec. 5.3

Top speed, mph 138

Under the skin, the 1968–1982 generation Corvette wasn't significantly different than the classic '63–'67 series. But a curvaceous new fiberglass body lent it a fresh personality and 435-hp 427-cid V-8s made it a ferocious predator. Despite such flaws as poor engine cooling and a finicky pop-up windshield wiper panel, sales were stronger than ever. The Stingray name returned for '69 after a year's absence, but now as one word. Pictured is one of 2722 'Vettes with the triple-carb 435-hp L71 427 built for '69, the last year this engine was available. The side exhausts were a $147 option.

CHEVROLET CORVETTE ZR1

*C*orvettes traditionally delivered world-class performance at middle-class prices. But this! This was acceleration, top speed, and braking to rival the upper-echelon exotics. Fans christened it King of the Hill. *Car and Driver* dubbed it the "Corvette from Hell." Chevrolet labeled it the ZR1.

ZR1 actually was the name of an option package that nearly doubled the price of a $32,000 base Corvette coupe. It debuted for 1990 after months of delays and breathless magazine previews. Dealers got $100,000 for early examples and Chevy got an image boost during a period in which it was being outsold—and GM was being outearned—by arch-rival Ford.

Planning for a super 'Vette began shortly after the third-generation model debuted for 1984. After considering a variety of homegrown turbo powerplants, Chevy got Britain's Lotus to design a sophisticated naturally aspirated V-8. Dubbed the LT5 and built by Mercury Marine in Oklahoma, the all-alloy dohc 32-valve 5.7-liter had 375 hp, 130 more than Corvette's base ohv 5.7, and came with a console-mounted

"valet key" so trepidacious owners could run it at part power. The ZR1 package included a six-speed manual, electronic adjustable suspension, and fatter rear tires.

From the start, there was grumbling that ZR1s were not visually distinct enough. They had wider rear fenders, but for '91 all Corvettes adopted the ZR1's convex tail panel and square taillamps. In '92, the gap in usable performance narrowed when base 'Vettes upgraded to the 300-hp LT1 V-8. Chevy responded for '93 by boosting the LT5 to 405 bhp, which cut 0–60 time by 0.2 seconds and added six mph in top speed compared to the original ZR1.

For all its spectacular performace, the ZR1 was a Corvette. It had gimmicky instrumentation, a pitlike interior, and workmanship at odds with its price. But what impressed as much as its ability to act savage was the ZR1's willingness to be sedate. "Even 179-mph cars spend most of their time coping with everyday traffic," wrote *Car and Driver*'s Csaba Csere, "and I can't think of another car this fast that does it this well."

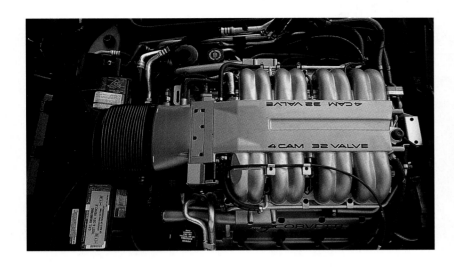

Chevrolet Corvette ZR1
1990–1995

Wheelbase, in. 96.2

Weight, lbs. 3529

Price $68,000

Engine dohc V-8

Displacement liters/cu. in. 5.7/350

Fuel system Fuel injection

Horsepower @ rpm 405 @ 5800

Torque @ rpm 385 @ 5200

Transmission 6-speed manual

Performance

0–60 mph, sec. 4.7

Top speed, mph 179

Chevrolet turned to its sports-car for an image boost and wasn't let down. The ZR1 set enthusiasts awhirl and prompted some to pay way over sticker for early examples. What they got was the fastest production 'Vette ever. GM's Lotus subsidiary designed a new V-8 that retained Chevy's 5.7-liter size, but added dual cams, high-tech induction, all-aluminum construction, and lots of horsepower. The interior was stock except for a "valet key" on the console that dialed the engine back to half power. The ZR1's only real styling change from ordinary Corvettes was its wider tail, which wasn't difference enough to some. Still, the King of the Hill fulfilled its mission. Its performance could be tame or titanic, and it was a great image builder. ZR1 was really an option package and 6939 were installed over the car's six-year run.

CHEVROLET CORVETTE

With a small-block Chevy V-8 in its nose, two seats in its cabin, and a hey-lookit-me fiberglass body, the fifth-generation Corvette was unmistakably part of a proud 43-year history. But it also was so fresh it seemed more reborn than redesigned. In fact, the '97 contained more never-before-used components than the very first Corvette.

Fans focussed first on the new look, a slippery semi-exotic coupe (convertible due for '98) with a whiff of mid-engine proportioning. Hidden headlamps recalled the '63 Sting Ray, side vents evoked bodyside hollows that appeared in '56, and quad taillamps continued a tradition begun in '61. Modern thinking was evident in the brief overhangs and low cowl. The body was longer than the '96's by a half inch, but wheelbase was stretched by 8.3 inches and the track was significantly wider, by 4.3 inches in front and by 3 in back, making the rear equal to the ZR1's. Inside was a roomier cockpit with a dual-cove dashboard inspired by the classic 1963–67 design. Gauges eschewed a digital/analog mishmash for circular numbers and needles.

Engineers got their kicks beneath the skin, starting with a new perimeter-frame chassis of seamless tubular steel vastly stronger than any previous Corvette structure. Gone was an independent rear suspension that, by rely-ing on the rear axles for its upper links, transmitted powertrain vibration through the chassis. Its replacement was a true double-wishbone setup segregated from the powertrain. Handling was improved and slightly narrower tires could be used, to the benefit of directional stability.

Power came from a clean-sheet redesign of the sacrosanct pushrod 5.7-liter V-8, now rendered in aluminum and linked via a six-speed gearbox or four-speed automatic with a rear transaxle. Moving the transmission to the back of the car created a 50/50 weight balance and freed up needed footwell space.

A driver senses rebirth from the first turn of the key, and not just because the ignition switch is off the steering column and back on the dashboard. The V-8 resounds from four central tailpipes rather than reverberating through the structure. There's a new sense of command because more of the road ahead is revealed by the low cowl, and the tail now stays the course through a bumpy turn. This is a disciplined high-performance machine.

Bettering a 12-year-old design and a rear suspension that dated from 1963 was simple. Making the new Corvette a great sports car—and keeping it a Corvette—was the achievement.

Just the fifth major redesign in Corvette history resulted in the "newest" 'Vette ever. The exterior of the 1997 model conjured up cues from Corvettes past, but presented them in one of the most aerodynamic shapes on the road. The interior returned to classic round analog gauges and presented a commanding view of the road thanks to a lower cowl. Called the LS1, the new all-alloy 5.7-liter V-8 teamed with a rear-transaxle to furnish a 50/50 weight balance and more cabin space.

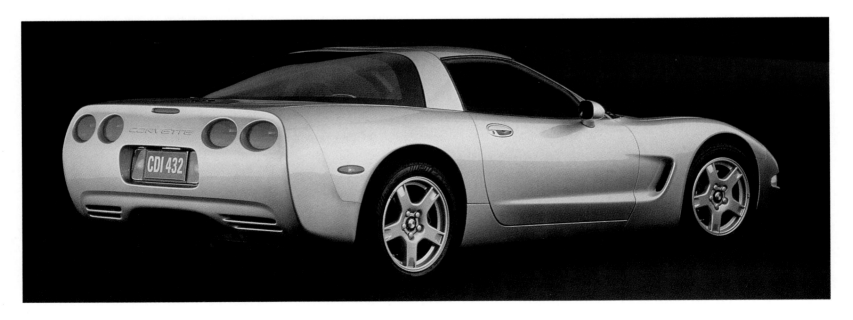

DATSUN 240Z

*I*f you're an automaker with something to prove, nothing gets attention like a sports car. Just as the Corvette helped erase Chevrolet's stodgy image in the 1950s, the 240Z bowed late in 1969 to serve notice that Datsun—or rather, parent Nissan Motors—was capable of more exciting things than small economy sedans.

Nissan was no stranger to sports cars, having offered its small British-style Fairlady roadsters since 1959. The 240Z was far more ambitious: a virtual poor man's Jaguar E-type packed with amenities, all at a bargain price—initially just $3500. Though called a Fairlady in Japan, the 240 owed nothing to its roadster forebears. Count Albrecht Goertz, of BMW 507 fame, penned a crisp hatchback coupe with seating for two in a cozy cockpit. Beneath this unitized structure was a classic all-independent suspension, anti-roll bars front and rear, and unassisted rack-and-pinion steering. Brakes were good-sized front discs and rear drums.

Power came from a single-cam inline-six out of a big Nissan sedan, sized near 2.4 liters (hence the export model name) and hooked to a four-speed gearbox (optional three-speed automatic from 1971). Despite unusual sports-car standard features including radio, reclining seats, full carpeting, and flow-through ventilation, curb weight was a svelte 2355 lbs. The Z was speedy despite fairly modest power. *Road & Track* in its initial test lauded the "combination of styling, performance and handling far ahead of anything else under $4000 . . . [W]e expect to see the Datsun establish a market of its own, one which will force other makers to [respond]."

Others did, because the 240Z sold like nickel beer: up to 50,000 a year in the U.S. alone by 1973. Club racers quickly embraced it, and Datsun won a barrel of trophies. The Z lost power and poise with the compromised 260 and 280 models of 1973–78. Two more redesigns produced what one wag called the "Ford LTD of sports cars" before Nissan got back to basics with the 300ZX of 1990. But none had the particular appeal of the original, which is among the very few Japanese cars considered a modern classic.

Datsun 240Z
1970–1973

Wheelbase, in. 90.7

Weight, lbs. 2355

Price $3500

Engine sohc I-6

Displacement liters/cu. in. 2.4/146

Fuel system 2 x 1 bbl. carburetors

Horsepower @ rpm 150 @ 6000

Torque @ rpm 148 @ 4400

Transmission 4-speed manual

Performance

0–60 mph, sec. 8.7

Top speed, mph 122

The 240Z showed the Japanese could build a wonderful sports car and compelled rivals to improve or die. The original two-seat coupe was marketed by Nissan as the Fairlady Z in Japan and by its U.S. arm, Datsun, as the 240Z. It delivered performance, looks, and features previously unavailable at such a reasonable price. Styling by German Albrecht Goertz had Jaguar overtones, and the cabin featured clean sports-car design, lots of features, and good materials. Underneath was an all-independent suspension and a strong, reliable ohc 2.4-liter six. The model shown has the optional automatic transmission. Subsequent 260Z and 280Z models reflected displacement boosts and the restyled disco-era 280ZX/300ZX offered 2+2 seating, but none could match the 240Z's verve.

DeTOMASO PANTERA

As Alejandro deTomaso, an Argentine living in Italy, struggled to build a petite four-cylinder sports car called the Vallelunga, Ford's wildly popular 1964½ Mustang arrived to make Lee Iacocca an American business icon. Five years later, this automotive David and Goliath teamed to create the world's first affordable mid-engine supercar.

The DeTomaso Pantera couldn't have happened without Alejandro's second car, the Mangusta (Italian for "mongoose"). Announced in 1966, it was a brawny high-speed mid-engine coupe with a "backbone" chassis and gorgeous looks. Alejandro liked Ford engines, so he chose the same 289-cid V-8 that was making Ford's racing GT40 a threat to Ferrari. Although a handful to drive and wildly impractical, the Mangusta generated 400 orders and Alessandro realized his dream of becoming a viable carmaker.

With this newfound prosperity, DeTomaso Automobili bought the famous Ghia coachworks, which employed young American-born designer Tom Tjaarda. By early 1969, Tjaarda, along with chassis wizard Giampaolo Dallara and body engineer Venanzio Di Biase, were working on a "new Mangusta." DeTomaso had recently met Iacocca,

soon to be Ford president, and they agreed to sell the new model through U.S. Lincoln-Mercury dealers. Trouble was, it hadn't been engineered for the 5000-unit annual volume Iacocca envisioned, prompting a crash redesign completed just in time for the Pantera (Panther) to star at the 1970 New York Auto Show.

It was basically a Mangusta with a tuned Ford 351 V-8, a more conventional Ghia-built body, and styling that Tjaarda termed "aggressive, almost beastlike . . . yet refined." The Pantera was beastly to drive, and far from refined, with numerous early quality snags. Workmanship improved under Ford's hand, and demand was strong thanks to a sub-$10,000 starting price—sensationally low for a Latin "exoticar." An easily serviced drivetrain and Ford's full new-car warranty enhanced the appeal.

U.S. sales ended after 1973. New federal regulations would have dictated a costly redesign, something Ford couldn't justify at such low volumes. The car survived in Europe through the mid-1990s, however, becoming faster, more civilized, and better built. Though far from perfect even at the end, the Pantera made history on its own terms. That's a sports-car great.

DeTomaso Pantera
1971–1973

Wheelbase, in. 98.4

Weight, lbs. 3155

Price $9000

Engine ohv V-8

Displacement liters/cu. in. 5.7/351

Fuel system 1 x 4 bbl. carburetor

Horsepower @ rpm 310 @ 5400

Torque @ rpm 380 @ 3400

Transmission 5-speed manual

Performance

0–60 mph, sec. 6.8

Top speed, mph 129

The coolest sports-car hybrid of the 1970s put a rumbling 351-cid Ford V-8 in a crisply styled Italian body from Alejandro deTomaso. It was sold through Lincoln-Mercury dealers and was the world's first affordable mid-engine exotic. The Pantera (Panther) survived into the 1990s as a bespoiled parody of this smooth original.

DODGE VIPER RT/10

*F*orget those modern high-performance sports cars that loaf to the supermarket and lap Sebring with equal proficiency. The Viper roadster's got a dual personality, all right: bad and badder.

That's intentional, of course. This is Chrysler's reborn 427 AC/Shelby Cobra, a pure two-seater with rear-wheel drive and a good ol' overhead-valve engine. No turbocharging. No anti-lock brakes. No electronic suspension. No traction control. No air bags. Not even real side windows. Just irresistible force.

A couple of Chrysler Corporation "car guys"—President Bob Lutz (jet pilot, Cobra-replica owner) and design chief Tom Gale (unabashed street-rodder)—say they simply decided one day in 1988 to build the damn thing. People waved deposit checks over the concept version at the '89 Detroit auto show, and within 11 months, "Team Viper" had a running prototype. A hand-built example paced the 1991 Indy 500 driven by none other than Carroll Shelby, whom Lutz and Gale credit with helping to conceptualize the car. Production Vipers were ready by 1992.

Chrysler turned to Lamborghini, its Italian subsidiary at the time, for an aluminum adaptation of the Dodge Ram pickup's 8.0-liter V-10; it was rated at 375 hp. The plastic-composite body and space-frame chassis were new design technologies to the Detroit automaker, while the all-independent suspension, 13-inch brake discs, and 17-inch steamroller tires were logical applications.

On the road, everything about the Viper seemed exaggerated, from the gasps elicited by its bawdy bodywork, to the endless-torque acceleration, to unpredictable handling at the limit. Side exhausts honored the Cobra but created flesh-singeing door sills and emitted a muted rasp.

Production purposely trailed demand, but by 1996, Dodge saw the need for a slightly more civilized coupe version, and the 450-hp GTS was born. The '96 roadster grew to 415 hp and adopted the coupe's mellifluent rear exhaust outlets; '97s got its dual air bags, rollup windows, and improved suspension. But not to worry, it's still as refreshingly, obsessively single-minded as the original.

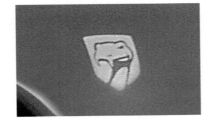

Dodge Viper RT/10
1992–

Wheelbase, in. 96.2

Weight, lbs. 3445

Price $61,200

Engine ohv V-10

Displacement liters/cu. in. 8.0/488

Fuel system Fuel injection

Horsepower @ rpm 415 @ 5200

Torque @ rpm 488 @ 3600

Transmission 6-speed manual

Performance

0–60 mph, sec. 4.4

Top speed, mph 163

Car nuts within Chrysler's hierarchy hankered to produce an AC/Shelby Cobra for the 1990s and with spiritual guidance from Carroll Shelby himself, created the Viper. It's a high-powered, low-frills sports car. The original 1992–1996 roadster didn't have rollup windows or outside door handles, much less air bags. The enormous V-10 engine originated with the Dodge Ram pickup but was rendered in aluminum for the Viper by Lamborghini. For '96, rear-exit exhaust replaced side-mounted pipes and a GTS coupe was added. This car displays one of the unique paint schemes available on the '96 roadsters.

FERRARI 166MM BARCHETTA

*S*ports-car manufacturers typically race to promote their road cars. Enzo Ferrari built road cars to finance his consuming passion: racing. Of course, in the sports car's golden age, race cars *were* road cars. That's the magic of the 166MM.

It was the first Ferrari built in volume and, with victories at LeMans and other top venues, the first to show the world Enzo's genius. Ferrari was not an engineer or a designer, but the cars created by his craftsmen had the hot-blooded spirit he acquired as a racing driver and team manager for Alfa Romeo in the 1920s and '30s. The first cars to bear his name were a trio of 1947 roadsters called the Type 125. He built 39 more cars through 1949, first the Type 159, then the 166. As with all early Ferraris, the type designations reflected the cubic-centimeter displacement of a single engine cylinder.

The MM suffix celebrated a 166's victory in the Mille Miglia, the grueling 1000-mile Italian road race. The letters were unveiled late in '48 on a 166 roadster with an evocative new aluminum body by the design house Touring. The shape influenced sports-car styling worldwide and looked to Italians like a little boat, or *barchetta* (bar-KET-ta). The

underpinnings were relatively unadventurous: a robust frame of oval tubing, independent front suspension, live rear axle, lever-type shocks, and large drum brakes. The towering achievement was the engine, an aluminum ohc hemi-head 2.0-liter V-12 by former Alfa designer Gioacchino Colombo. With further development, this potent powerplant would be a Ferrari mainstay well into the 1960s. In the 166MM, it teamed with a non-synchro gearbox that had an unusual-for-the-day five speeds.

Being virtually hand-built, no two Ferraris were exactly alike during the company's first decade. All 166s had race-ready righthand drive, but there were two wheelbases (86.6 and 88.6 inches), bodies by different coachbuilders, even some coupes. The V-12 could have a single Weber or up to three, various compression ratios, and 90 hp to 140. The MM designation earmarked the competition cars, which won nearly everything in sight, including LeMans outright in '49, while slightly tamer "touring" versions wore the Inter label. In reality, most 166 Barchettas were raced at one time or another and all were formidable on road or track. The legend was born.

Ferrari 166MM Barchetta
1948–1953

Wheelbase, in. 86.6

Weight, lbs. 1880

Price $9500

Engine ohc V-12

Displacement liters/cu. in. 2.0/122

Fuel system 3 x 2 bbl. carburetors

Horsepower @ rpm 130 @ 7000

Torque @ rpm 117 @ 5000

Transmission 5-speed manual

Performance

0–60 mph, sec. 10.0

Top speed, mph 125

Ferrari's reputation as a builder of top sports cars began with the unassailable 166MM Barchetta. The body reminded Italians of a little boat, or barchetta, and influenced sports-car design worldwide. The MM suffix marked Ferrari's 1948 Mille Miglia win. While 166MMs were road cars, they were competition machines foremost. This example has the three-carb version of the 2.0-liter V-12 and raced in both the Targa Florio and Mille.

FERRARI 250 GT SWB BERLINETTA

*B*y the early 1960s, Ferrari sports cars were secure as the world's standard, a status authenticated in the crucible of racing. Names such as Ascari, Fangio, and Hawthorn rode them to world driving championships. The marque snared three Formula 1 manufacturer's titles. It won LeMans, Sebring, the Nürburgring, and scores of other events big and small.

The bridge from the pure racing cars that accounted for most of this success to the "civilized" customer Ferraris were Enzo's "competition GT" machines. These represented motoring's most romantic ideal—that a great road car could also be a winning race car. There were precious few such machines, and the last of them, arguably the greatest of all, was Ferrari's 250 GT SWB Berlinetta.

It debuted in 1959, its name telling the tale. "250" described the engine, a development of the original 1.5-liter Colombo V-12, now at 3.0 liters and 240 hp in standard tune and up to 295 in competition trim. "GT" meant Gran Turismo, a sports car capable of speeding its

occupants in comfort over long distances on public roads. "Berlinetta" was Ferrari's term for a closed two-seater designed to defend his name in GT-class racing. "SWB" stood for short wheelbase, and was what immortalized the car. Ferrari chopped 7.9 inches from the wheelbase of the 1956–1959 250 GT Berlinetta Tour de France to formulate a lighter, fabulously nimble new platform. Pininfarina condensed his latest coupe body around the new dimensions, creating what many consider his masterpiece.

Competition SWBs looked little different from Lusso or "luxury" models, but had a stiffer suspension, full aluminum body panels, plastic side windows, and less insulation.

At LeMans, the Nürburgring, Goodwood, Spa, Elkhart Lake, Bridgehampton, and elsewhere, SWBs won their classes and finished in the top five overall. So fine a dual-purpose sports car was the 250 GT SWB Berlinetta that Ferrari had to build two single-purpose cars to replace it. Romance would never be the same.

Ferrari 250 GT SWB Berlinetta 1959–1962

Wheelbase, in. 94.5

Weight, lbs. 2380

Price $14,000

Engine ohc V-12

Displacement liters/cu. in. 3.0/180

Fuel system 3 x 2 bbl. carburetors

Horsepower @ rpm 240 @ 7000

Torque @ rpm NA

Transmission 4-speed manual

Performance

0–60 mph, sec. 6.9

Top speed, mph 140

Ferrari lovers have room in their hearts for any number of stallions from Maranello, but the 250 GT SWB Berlinetta commands a special place of its own. Here was the last and probably best expression of the notion that a great sports car should be strong both on the road and at the track. This Ferrari was a champion no matter the setting. It used a trimmed-down race-proven chassis, hence the Short Wheelbase initials. The 3.0-liter version of Ferrari's mighty V-12 was treated to new cylinder heads from the Testa Rossa sports-racing car and made 240 hp in standard, tri-carb tune. Models intended primarily for competition got aluminum bodywork; road versions used some steel panels. Berlinetta described the 250 GT SWB coupe, and Pininfarina never surpassed its styling in form, detail, or proportion, which is saying a lot. Just 175 of these cars were produced.

FERRARI 250 GT SWB CALIFORNIA SPYDER

Spyder was Ferrari for convertible and, as the 250 GT SWB Berlinetta was Enzo's pinnacle dual-purpose coupe, the 250 GT SWB California Spyder was the *ne plus ultra* of his roadsters.

Like the SWB Berlinetta, with which it shared running gear, the SWB Spyder used the "short wheelbase" 250 GT Tour de France chassis and represented a new level in roadster performance. Ferrari's previous roadgoing cabriolets were intended as high-style touring cars and thus were derived from relatively tame coupes. That changed with the 250 GT California Spyder (1958–1963), which was based on the fast, competition-oriented Tour de France Berlinetta. The California name recognized the influence of wealthy American enthusiasts who clamored for speedy open Ferraris.

Enzo turned up the wick even more in May 1960 with the 250 GT SWB convertible. This was essentially a shortened version of that original California Spyder, but was quicker thanks to 50 lbs less weight and handled better thanks to 7.9 inches less wheelbase

and nearly 17 inches less overall length. It shared with the SWB Berlinetta an independent suspension and coil springs in front, live axle and tube shocks in back, and disc brakes all-around. Underhood was the great 3.0-liter Colombo V-12; it was docile in town, a dervish in the open, and an opera always. "There's no engine that begins to compare with it, that deserves mention in the same breath with the Ferrari V12," rhapsodized *Sports Cars Illustrated* in 1960.

All SWB Spyders had steel bodies with aluminum hoods and there was an optional removable hardtop. Styling was by Pininfarina, who in 1958 had changed his name from Battista "Pinin" Farina. It displayed the same gift of proportion that worked magic on the SWB Berlinetta. If anything, the SWB Spyder was even lovelier and had that same multiple personality, too. But while the SWB Spyder was not strictly intended for racing, it was raced and it was fast enough to pester Porsches, Corvettes, and even SWB Berlinettas.

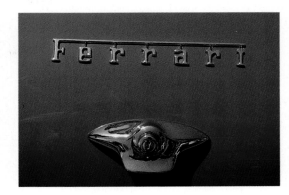

For beauty, driving enjoyment, and historical significance, there are few more coveted Ferraris than the 250 GT short wheelbase California Spyder. It applied open-air Pininfarina styling to the race-ready mechanicals of the SWB Berlinetta, including the immortal 3.0-liter V-12. Production ran from 1960 to early 1963 and numbered just 57 cars. As with the coupe, the body was assembled by the Italian coachbuilder Scaglietti. Most SWB Spyders had steel bodies with aluminum hoods and decklids, though a few versions that went racing had all-aluminum bodies.

Ferrari 250 GT SWB California Spyder 1960–1963

Wheelbase, in. 94.5

Weight, lbs. 2380

Price $14,000

Engine ohc V-12

Displacement liters/cu. in. 3.0/180

Fuel system 3 x 2 bbl. carburetors

Horsepower @ rpm 240 @ 7000

Torque @ rpm NA

Transmission 4-speed manual

Performance

0–60 mph, sec. 7.0

Top speed, mph 130

FERRARI 250 GTO

"*I*f there's a quintessential Ferrari, it could well be this sensational racing coupe," wrote automotive journalist Pete Lyons. And who's to argue? Not only did the 250 GTO have timeless styling and world-title performance, it embodied Enzo Ferrari at his most cunning.

Rule changes announced in 1961 mandated that starting in 1962, the prestigious World Manufacturers Championship would be contested by Grand Touring sports cars. Ferrari knew winning would require a car more aerodynamic than the 250 GT SWB Berlinetta, and, by 1960, had already started developing its successor. Bypassing Pininfarina, he set his own designers to conjure a slippery new shape on a beefed-up SWB platform. From their wind tunnel came a longer, lighter, low-nose aluminum body that introduced what became a staple of virtually every race car and of every car intended to look racy: the tail spoiler. This aero aid had just been invented by Ferrari's American test driver, Richie Ginther.

A 3.0-liter V-12 returned, but it was the full-out, six-carburetor, dry-sump competition engine from Ferrari's Testa Rossa sports-racer and

was hooked to a new five-speed gearbox. Instead of advancing to all-independent suspension, an improved version of the SWB's basic beam rear axle underpinnings was preserved. Enzo had spied a loophole in the rules, and was darting though it.

A manufacturer had to build 100 production examples of a GT to qualify it for competition. Ferrari had no intention of producing that many copies of this expensive new racer. So he convinced authorities that it was merely an evolution of the SWB, of which more than 100 had already been built. Even its name reinforced the ruse. GTO stood for Gran Turismo Omologato, *omologato* meaning "homologated," or an automobile recognized by racing rules-makers as a production car.

Unlike the dual-purpose 250 GT SWB, however, the GTO was stripped of every item that didn't make it go faster and was ill-suited to roadwork. Just 39 were built (three with 4.0-liter V-12s) and sure enough, won Enzo the coveted World Manufacturers Championship in '62, '63, and '64. Quintessential Ferrari, indeed.

Ferrari 250 GTO
1962–1964

Wheelbase, in. 94.5

Weight, lbs. 2474

Price $20,000

Engine ohc V-12

Displacement liters/cu. in. 3.0/180

Fuel system 6 x 2 bbl. carburetors

Horsepower @ rpm 300 @ 7400

Torque @ rpm 250 @ 5500

Transmission 5-speed manual

Performance

0–60 mph, sec. 5.8

Top speed, mph 176

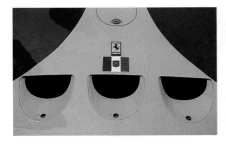

No cavallino is more respected than the 250 GTO. Voluptuous, uncompromising, and very fast, it was the last of Ferrari's front-engine competition cars. The name stems from its role as a "production" Gran Turismo that is omologato—homologated—or sanctioned to race. The aluminum 3.0-liter V-12 had six Webers and 100 hp per liter. The cockpit was a sporting tour de force. The GTO pictured is a fine example of the car's cagey persona. It's streetable, but has a racing history that includes Sebring, Daytona, and the Targa Florio. The colors reflect the nationality of its Swedish race driver and owner.

FERRARI 275 GTB/4

With the 250 GTO, Ferrari acknowledged that a single car could no longer fulfill the diverging demands of road and track. Where once the 250 GT SWB satisfied both needs, the GTO was now his racer, while a pretty new coupe, the 250 GT Berlinetta Lusso, carried the prancing horse on the highway. Trouble was, Enzo found the Lusso too pretty and, after making 350 of the elegant Pininfarina-styled two-seaters between 1962 and 1964, he moved on to the 275 GTB.

Pininfarina's work here was far less delicate, being instead a muscular shape that bespoke a newfound aggressiveness beneath the skin. Like the GTO and Lusso, the 275 GTB used the SWB chassis, but discarded the beam rear axle to become the first roadgoing Ferrari with all-independent suspension. It also was the first with a rear transaxle, a further boon to handling balance. Finally, the Colombo V-12 received its first displacement increase in 12 years, a boost to 3.3 liters that triggered the "275" designation. Bowing in 1964, the GTB (Berlinetta) had 275 hp at 7500 rpm, while its companion roadster, the 275 GTS

(Spyder), got 260 at 7000. Both had cabins of leather and wood, and suspensions of pleasing absorbency.

In 1966, came a 275 GTB with a small hood bulge that heralded new cylinder heads of two camshafts per bank—Ferrari's first dohc street engine. Called the GTB/4, it had 300 hp at a towering 8000 rpm and, with dry-sump lubrication to maintain oil pressure, invited strenuous driving. The factory never built a racing GTB/4, though, so its proving ground was the road. There, it was a lion among lambs.

In 1967, professional racer Jean-Pierre Beltoise covered 46 miles in 23 minutes in one on the French Autoroute, fighting Sunday traffic and stopping for tolls. He wrote of doing so "in complete safety and the greatest comfort, without having to once use the brakes hard and while carrying on a normal conversation with my passenger . . . It is, first and foremost, a serious and comfortable gran turismo, but it retains the lineage of a race car in the response of the engine and the quality of the handling. The 275 GTB/4 is one of the greatest automobiles created in our times."

Ferrari 275 GTB/4
1966–1967

Wheelbase, in. 94.5

Weight, lbs. 2663

Price $14,680

Engine dohc V-12

Displacement liters/cu. in. 3.3/200

Fuel system 6 x 2 bbl. carburetors

Horsepower @ rpm 300 @ 8000

Torque @ rpm NA

Transmission 5-speed manual

Performance

0–60 mph, sec. 6.2

Top speed, mph 155

Recognizing that he could no longer build a single car to satisfy the demands of both road and track, Ferrari in 1963 introduced the pretty 250 GT Berlinetta Lusso, which used the hot 250 GT SWB running gear, but in a more civilized package. For '64, he moved on to the 275 GTB. This car retained the SWB wheelbase, but had less-delicate styling and was the first touring Ferrari with an all-independent suspension and a rear transaxle. The aging but still wondrous Colombo V-12 was enlarged from 3.0 to 3.3 liters, and then in 1966 added dual overhead camshafts to redesignate the car the 275 GTB/4. A subtle hood bulge on the GTB/4 was the main visual change. Through 1967, Ferrari built about 650 GTB coupes and convertibles, 280 GTB/4 coupes, and 10 GTB/4 Spyders.

FERRARI 365 GTB/4 DAYTONA

*O*f all the photos *Road & Track* ran with its first test of the new Ferrari, one said it all. Dean Batchelor's shot showed a man's hands resting comfortably at nine and three, thumbs draped over the polished spokes of a wood-rimmed steering wheel. Clearly visible were the instruments. The tachometer's needle was lodged at 7000 rpm, the speedometer's pointer was parked on 180 mph. It was evident from the view through the windshield that this was on a public road.

Few envisioned an image of such speed and composure when the 365 GTB/4 Daytona was revealed late in 1968. Lamborghini had expanded the supercar frontier in 1966 with its mid-engine Miura and here was Ferrari, with plenty of mid-engine racing experience and with the just-launched midships V-6 Dino, replaying the old front-engine formula for his new flagship.

Enzo felt he owed the world no more explanation than to snap, "The horse does not push the cart, it pulls." But the Daytona was a *gran turismo*, not a competition car, and Ferrari knew the front-engine layout required fewer compromises than the mid-engine form. Building on the

proven wheelbase and 50/50 balance of the 275 GTB/4, he could provide an inviting coupe with a comfortable cabin and adequate luggage space.

Emissions concerns had forced him to enlarge his evergreen V-12, first to 4.0 liters, then, for the Daytona, to a magnificent four-cam 4.4. Pininfarina clothed it all in a new steel skin whose exaggerated long-hood, short-deck proportions were a hosanna to the front-engine faith. European versions had clear headlamp covers, but flip-up pods were used on U.S. cars to satisfy American lighting laws.

Steering, shifting, and clutch were heavy and, at nearly 3900 pounds with driver and fuel, the Daytona was not tossable. But it was tough. The factory built 15 competition versions for private teams, and they raced into the 1980s. Ferrari also produced about 115 roadsters so fetching they inspired some berlinetta owners to convert their cars. As for that famous photograph, the speedometer it pictured exaggerated the Daytona's top speed by about seven mph, but that was still five mph faster than the Miura. Some horse cart.

While rivals were turning to mid-engine designs for their supercars, Ferrari stubbornly clung to a time-tested formula. The strategy paid off in one of his most celebrated cars, the Daytona. The front-engine layout furnished familiar road manners and comfortable passenger accommodations, and allowed classic long-hood, short-deck styling. European versions had clear headlamp covers, as shown, but U.S. models resorted to flip-up lamp pods. All used an enormously energetic quad-cam V-12 with six twin-choke Webers. Production of road versions totaled 1400 Daytona coupes and 115 droptop spyders.

Ferrari 365 GTB/4 Daytona 1968–1973

Wheelbase, in. 94.5

Weight, lbs. 3600

Price $19,500

Engine dohc V-12

Displacement liters/cu. in. 4.4/286

Fuel system 6 x 2 bbl. carburetors

Horsepower @ rpm 352 @ 7500

Torque @ rpm 315 @ 5500

Transmission 5-speed manual

Performance

0–60 mph, sec. 5.9

Top speed, mph 173

FERRARI 512 BBi

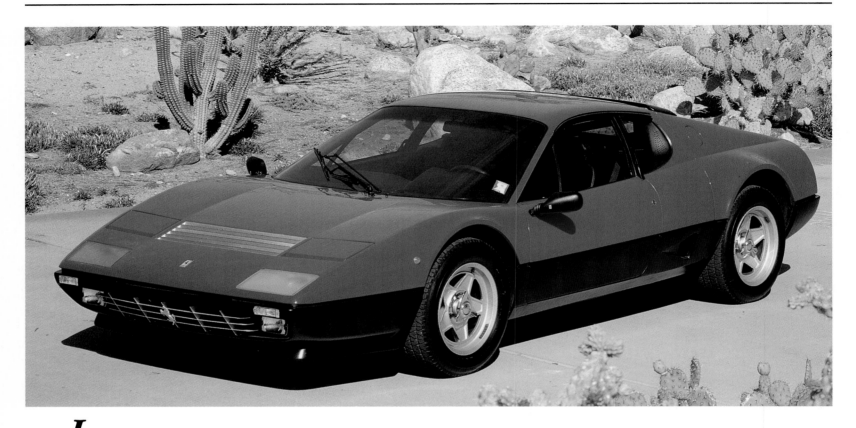

*I*t was time to put the cart before the horse. By the early 1970s, competitors were using mid-engine exotics to chip away at Ferrari's prestige. Ferrari fought back with the Boxer.

Ferrari's front-engine obsession had weakened in 1962 with the mid-engine 250 LM, ostensibly a dual-purpose GT but really a racing coupe that won LeMans in 1965. The first mid-engine road Ferrari was the 1969 Dino, a small V-6 coupe named after Enzo's late son, but it never bore Ferrari badging. Lamborghini had debuted its V-12 Miura for 1966, and its outrageous Countach was on display for 1971, by which time Maserati, Porsche, and Lotus had joined the mid-engine mealy.

Ferrari showed his first midships supercar, the 365 GT4/Berlinetta Boxer, at the 1971 Turin show. By the time production began in 1973, it was known simply as the Boxer. It replaced the Daytona atop the Ferrari line and, like the Daytona, it had a 4.4-liter 12-cylinder engine. But its cylinders were horizontally opposed, "boxing" each other. The flat-12 was located longitudinally behind the two-seat cockpit and was compact

enough to fit above the transaxle. The new flagship's tube frame was reinforced with sheetmetal. Its lower bodywork including bumpers was fiberglass, with a mix of steel and aluminum panels above.

Smog and noise laws prompted an increase to 5.0 liters in 1977 and a new name, the 512 BB. The engine retained four three-throat Webers and was still factory-rated at 360 hp, but now at 6200 rpm, not 7000, and it had more torque. Ferrari also addressed shortcomings of the first-generation Boxer with improved seats, slicker shifting, dry-sump lubrication, standard air conditioning to combat the abundance of cabin heat, wider rear tires to keep the tail in line at the limit, and a chin spoiler to quell front-end lift. Fuel injection arrived during 1981, dropping the 5.0 to 340 hp and changing the name to 512 BBi. Both 512s were heavier and slightly slower than the original Boxer, but were easier to drive.

Ferrari had come reluctantly to the mid-engine fray, but when he arrived it was with a car that translated the new layout into the grand-touring idiom without surrendering a sliver of performance to its rivals.

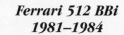

Ferrari 512 BBi
1981–1984

Wheelbase, in. 98.4

Weight, lbs. 3500

Price $120,000

Engine dohc flat-12

Displacement liters/cu. in. 5.0/301

Fuel system Fuel injection

Horsepower @ rpm 340 @ 6000

Torque @ rpm 333 @ 4200

Transmission 5-speed manual

Performance

0–60 mph, sec. 5.3

Top speed, mph 175

Ferrari had built mid-engine racing cars and a Dino-badged mid-engine V-6 coupe, but he resisted the midships wave until 1973, when the 365 GT4/Berlinetta Boxer hit the road. Its Boxer name was derived from the flat V-12 engine, originally 4.4 liters, then enlarged to 5.0 for the 1977 512 BB. An "i" suffix signified its 1981 adoption of fuel injection. This was among the most refined of the era's midships supercars, but was as fast as any of them.

FERRARI 308 GTS

While image demanded that Ferrari offer full-bore super-cars such as the Boxer, Enzo himself retained a taste for lighter fare, an appetite he satisfied enthusiastically during the mid-engine era.

His V-6 Dinos of 1969–1974 were agile and quick; the 195-hp 2.4-liter 246 GT did 148 mph. The larger Bertone-styled Dino 308 GT4 introduced in 1972 could hit 152 mph, but it was an anomaly: a mid-engine 2+2. In 1975, Ferrari finally mated the mid-engine form with serious power in a true sports-car package.

The breakthrough was the 308 GTB. As on the 308 GT4, the model number denoted a 3.0-liter four-cam V-8, transversely mounted ahead of the rear axle and topped by four twin-choke Webers. Rated horsepower was 205 at 6600 rpm. Chassis was much like the Dino 246's, including the nimble 92.1-inch wheelbase. And Pininfarina was back with a styling landmark. The 308's sensuous curves, hidden headlamps, flying-buttress fastback, and neat Kamm-style rump set the pattern for Ferrari's volume offerings through the rest of the cen-tury. Its bodyside wedges, which formed functional scoops, were an element that would appear on several future models as well. Fiberglass was used for the bodyshell, and though quality was high, Ferrari buyers weren't accustomed to "plastic cars," so steel con-struction took over in 1977. That coincided with introduction of the targa-top 308 GTS.

Emissions forced adoption of fuel injection for 1981, and 1982 brought a new Quattrovalvolve V-8 with four valves per cylinder, lifting output to 230 hp at 6800 rpm. With minor styling tweaks came the 328 GTB/GTS, which bowed in 1985 with a 270-hp 3.2 V-8 and was fol-lowed in 1990 by the 296-hp 3.4-liter 348 GTB/GTS. Crowning the series in 1993 was the 348 Spyder, the first two-seat Ferrari convertible since the Daytona Spyder.

Athletic and exciting, the 308 GTB/GTS is today prized for its classic carbureted V-8 unfettered by power-sapping emissions equipment, and especially for its trendsetting purity of line.

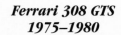

Ferrari 308 GTS
1975–1980

Wheelbase, in. 92.1

Weight, lbs. 3085

Price $28,500

Engine dohc V-8

Displacement liters/cu. in. 3.0/179

Fuel system 4 x 2 bbl. carburetors

Horsepower @ rpm 205 @ 6600

Torque @ rpm 181 @ 5000

Transmission 5-speed manual

Performance

0–60 mph, sec. 6.4

Top speed, mph 154

With its two-seat configuration, sensuous Pininfarina lines, mid-engine form, and V-8 powertrain, the 308 GTB and GTS set the tone for Ferrari's "volume" offerings through the balance of the century. This targa-top GTS "spyder" body style followed the original GTB "berlinetta" coupe by two years. A true convertible descendent arrived in 1993 as the 348 Spyder.

FERRARI 288 GTO

*"T*he car swept up in a flurry of exhaust bark, induction whistles, ignition rasps, cam whirs and with a sizzling of valves." So said *Car* magazine in August 1984 upon its first encounter with the latest Ferrari. This behavior was merely the stomping of a thoroughbred in its stall. The car actually ran without fuss, and even had a comfortable air conditioned cabin. Indeed, said *Car and Driver*, "This little Ferrari feels as if it would be perfectly comfortable delivering kids to school . . . at least until you drop your right boot. Then a 747 rolls up from the rear and leans against the bumper with four engines' worth of takeoff thrust."

To casual eyes, the new coupe was a 308 GTB. But only the steel doors were shared, and there were enormous differences elsewhere. The most significant distinction was on the tail, where a small badge read GTO. Ferrari does not bestow these letters lightly. The 288 GTO *was* a Gran Turismo Omologato—a grand touring car homologated for racing, in this case the just-announced Group B series for street-legal two-seaters.

Homologation required construction of 200 production examples.

That was too few to justify a new body-design program, though Pininfarina did pay homage to the original 250 GTO with bold fender vents and a ducktail spoiler. Racing really did mold this car.

Four-wheel drive and anti-lock brakes were dismissed as highway frills. The engine was a dohc 32-valve V-8 of 2.8 liters, a size that allowed turbocharging under Group B rules. A pair of small Japanese-made turbos was chosen because two responded quicker than a single large one. The engine sat longitudinally in the steel-tube chassis with the transaxle behind, simplifying quick gearset changes for racing. Finally, there were exotic composite materials: fiberglass body panels, a Kevlar hood, a Kevlar and carbon-fiber roof, a firewall of Kevlar, Nomex, and aluminum honeycomb. Though the mechanicals were heavier and the car longer and wider than the 308 GTB, the 288 GTO weighed 205 lbs less.

Alas, Group B disbanded before it could race. But Ferrari had resurrected the dual-purpose GT using the latest technology and materials. The 288 GTO was obedient and energetic, beautiful and blindingly quick. It was a thoroughbred.

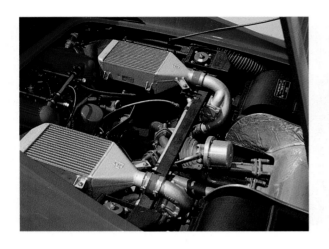

In 1984, Ferrari revived a hallowed name for its new road/racing car: GTO. It echoed the look of the 308 GTB, but was wider and used such advanced structural materials as Kevlar and Nomex. The midships V-8 displaced 2.8 liters (hence the 288 name), had two small turbochargers, and 394 hp; race versions were expected to make 600 hp. Designed as a sports-racer, the GTO needed a cabin for two, plus gauges, lights, ground clearance, and windshield wipers legal for road use. Unfortunately, its racing series dissolved before the 288 GTO could turn a wheel in anger. Production totaled 220 cars over four years.

Ferrari 288 GTO
1984–1987

Wheelbase, in. 96.5

Weight, lbs. 2880

Price $125,000

Engine Twin turbo dohc V-8

Displacement liters/cu. in. 2.8/174

Fuel system Fuel injection

Horsepower @ rpm 394 @ 7000

Torque @ rpm 366 @ 3800

Transmission 5-speed manual

Performance

0–60 mph, sec. 5.0

Top speed, mph 175

FERRARI 512TR

*S*upercars are the bullies of the sports-car world, menacing with size, shape, and sheer speed. One-upped in this war of intimidation by Lamborghini's ever-more unnerving Countach, Ferrari replaced the Boxer and trumped the competition by evoking what few could match: a racing heritage.

Between 1958 and 1962 , Ferrari won LeMans four times and the World Sports Car Championship three times with its Testa Rossa sports-racers. The name meant red head and was inspired by the crimson color of their camshaft covers. The Testarossa unveiled in 1984 was a pure highway machine linked to those storied Ferraris by the red crackle finish of its cylinder heads.

This new supercar replayed the Boxer's chassis design and midships 5.0-liter flat-12, though with four valves per cylinder and 380 hp. More impressive was the fabulous new Pininfarina styling. It was a low wedge, larger yet lighter than the Boxer and, at an imposing 77.8 inches, wider than all rivals save the Countach itself. The Testarossa had

more cargo and passenger space than the Lambo, and locating a pair of radiators ahead of the rear wheels eliminated the plumbing that overheated the Boxer's cabin. Serving the radiators were huge bodyside vents that met European intake-size restrictions with a series of thin horizontal ribs. Criticized at first, Pininfarina's strakes soon became a copied styling cue. A single outrigger mirror on the windshield pillar was the final avant-garde touch on this $115,000 exotic.

Revisions for 1992 shortened the name to 512TR and created the definitive Testarossa. Output climbed to a snarling 421 hp, top speed rose to 187 mph from 176, and 0–60 mph came 1.5 seconds sooner. Handling improved via a stiffer chassis and wider tires on larger wheels, lovely 18-inch alloys that made the car look sleeker and showed off its huge new disc brakes. Luggage space and ergonomics were better, too. A 1994 facelift that eliminated the retractable headlamps was less successful. Horsepower jumped to 440, but Ferrari now called the car the 512M, relegating its red head once again to the pages of history.

The Testarossa assumed the mantle of Ferrari's flagship in 1984. Its cabin was larger and more comfortable than the Boxer's and its luggage capacity was greater. With crimson-painted cylinder heads on its horizontally opposed 12-cylinder engine, it was literally a testa rossa: red head. The name first described a late-1950s Ferrari sports-racing car and was last used on the facelifted 1992 512TR (shown). The huge side vents fed air to the radiators and their "cheese-slicer" grilles helped meet European laws limiting the size of bodyside openings. Function as automotive art; that's Ferrari.

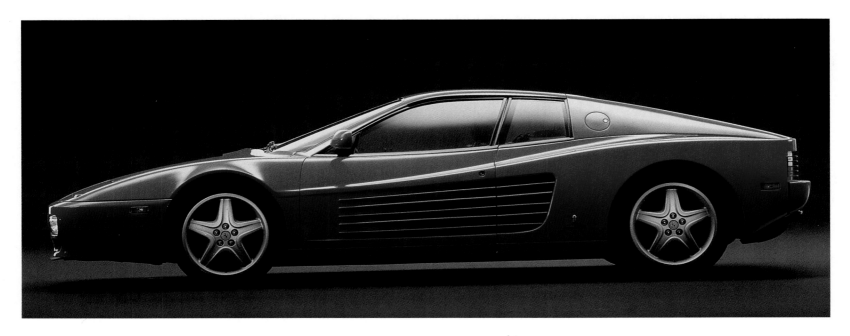

FERRARI F40

*N*o one present could help but be deeply moved by the figure of 89-year-old Enzo Ferrari unveiling this new and extremely special automobile. It was July 1987, at his Maranello headquarters, and the car was the F40.

The name commemorated Ferrari's 40th year as an automaker and those who drove the F40 had no trouble labeling it the best sports car of the day. That was distinct from the other leading speed machine of the moment, the refined, all-wheel-drive Porsche 959, which was the best all-around performance car.

The mid-engine two-seat F40 was elemental in a way Ferraris had not been since the early days. It made few concessions to comfort in the traditional sense. There were no interior door handles, only primitive pull cords. Side windows were sliding Plexiglas panes. Outside mirrors didn't adjust from inside the car. The foot pedals were drilled bare metal and the bucket seats were thin shells clad in fire-resistant Nomex and sized to fit different physiques. There was no carpeting. The

dashboard was covered in cloth. Feeble air conditioning battled the cockpit's poor ventilation.

This was not a race car but it brought racing technology to the road. Molded carbon-fiber and Kevlar panels were bonded to large-diameter steel tubing for a strong yet featherweight chassis. Fuel was stored in two rubber-cell tanks. The suspension adjusted to lower the car at speed. A body of light aerospace plastics generated its own downforce. There was no anti-lock system, no traction control. A tuned version of the GTO's twin-turbo V-8 wooshed 478 hp to Formula 1-width rear wheels. The F40 was as large as the contemporary Testarossa but weighed 700 lbs less and had 98 hp more.

"By a huge margin, it is the most exciting, exhilarating car I have driven in 35 years," wrote Roger Bell in *Car* magazine.

It was as if Enzo knew this would be his last Ferrari and wanted it to be the sort of feral wonder that made his name in the first place. It was. He died on August 14, 1988.

The F40 was the last Ferrari built while Enzo Ferrari was alive and it took the great man back to his automotive roots. This was no grand touring machine, but a sports car shorn of amenities and packed with power. The chassis used carbon fiber and Kevlar, and the lightweight plastic body was shaped to provide aerodynamic downforce necessary to travel within a blink of 200 mph. Fuel was stored in two rubber-celled tanks and fire-resistant Nomex served as the upholstery. Pull cords opened the doors, and there was no carpeting. Anti-lock brakes were not offered, the F40 relying instead on huge discs and the driver's ability. Lifting the louvered tail section revealed a 2.9-liter twincam V-8 with dual turbos and 478 hp. The F40 was the best unadulterated sports car of its day.

Ferrari F40
1988–1991

Wheelbase, in. 96.5

Weight, lbs. 3018

Price $470,000

Engine Twin turbo dohc V-8

Displacement liters/cu. in. 2.9/179

Fuel system Fuel injection

Horsepower @ rpm 478 @ 7000

Torque @ rpm 424 @ 4500

Transmission 5-speed manual

Performance

0–60 mph, sec. 3.8

Top speed, mph 196

FERRARI F50

Where the F40 united Ferrari's untamed past with its carbon-fiber future, the F50 took it to sport motoring's cutting edge. Formula 1 technology was now in the thrilling service of the highway driver.

"Compared to the twice-as-expensive and comfort-engineered McLaren F-1, the F50's mission is to deliver the most intense driving experience possible," said *Motor Trend*. "It does that beautifully."

The F50's guiding principles are strong but lightweight construction and enormous power—a blend possible only through real racing engineering. The "chassis" is actually a carbon-fiber tub weighing just 225 lbs. The engine and suspension are mounted to it. The suspension locates its dampers and springs at the center of the car and links them to the wheels via pushrods, like an open-wheel racing car. It also adjusts electronically depending on lateral forces, steering angle, and body attitude.

The 4.7-liter V-12 is a version of the 3.5 V-12 in Ferrari's 1989–90 Formula 1 racer and along with the six-speed transmission is a load-bearing component, as in the track car. It has five valves per cylinder (three intake, two exhaust), 11.3:1 compression, and pulls smoothly from 1500 rpm to its 9000-rpm redline. Above 4500 rpm, its scream is that of an F1 machine. "Alain Prost would find the noise familiar," wrote journalist Luca Ciferri. Almost as impressive is the race-car-like stopping power. Discs, 14 inches in diameter in front and 13 in the rear, are devoid of anti-lock control or, like the steering, even power assist.

The Pininfarina-designed body is of carbon fiber, Kevlar, and Nomex honeycomb, and a removable roof turns it from roadster to coupe. The shape of the belly creates a vacuum that sucks the car to the road. Hood "nostrils" extract air to create downforce. The leather-covered carbon-fiber seats come in regular and large; air conditioning is the only amenity.

This is the most expensive roadgoing Ferrari ever and just 349 are to be built. Buyers, each of whom gets a photo album of their car's assembly, will find the F50 easier to drive, better handling, and more comfortable than its spiritual predecessor, the race-ready F40. And around Ferrari's 1.8-mile test track, they'll find it almost two seconds faster.

Ferrari F50
1995–

Wheelbase, in. 101.6

Weight, lbs. 2712

Price $519,245

Engine dohc V-12

Displacement liters/cu. in. 4.7/288

Fuel system Fuel injection

Horsepower @ rpm 513 @ 8500

Torque @ rpm 347 @ 6500

Transmission 6-speed manual

Performance

0–60 mph, sec. 3.2

Top speed, mph 202

Raw excitement is the F50's assignment. Mission accomplished. The costliest roadgoing Ferrari ever brings genuine Formula 1 technology to the street. Its engine is an enlarged version of Ferrari's racing V-12 and produces more power per liter than any naturally aspirated production engine in history. In tandem with the transmission, it acts as a chassis member. Competition-proven carbon-fiber construction, inboard suspension components, and ground-force aerodynamics are part of the $519,245 package. So is a removable top that turns the F50 roadster into a cozy coupe. This isn't a racing car, but it feels like one.

FERRARI F355

*W*hile specialty sports cars such as the F50 captured headlines, Ferrari was busy developing "volume" models that by any measure were among the marque's best autos ever. The handsome 456GT 2+2 coupe of 1995 revived the classic front-engine V-12 layout, while the F355 bowed in 1994 to carry the mid-engine sports-car mantle.

Debuting as the GTB coupe and GTS targa, the F355 clearly descended from the 308 and was prettier and more powerful than its immediate predecessor, the 348. Its new 40-valve V-8 made 107 hp per liter, second only to the F50 as the highest specific output ever in a naturally aspirated production car. Veteran journalist Paul Frere praised it as "probably the best sports car engine ever made."

The F355 reprised the 348's anti-lock braking system, but supplanted its five-speed gearbox with a six speed and added power steering and dual air bags. Handling was better thanks to an electronically adjustable suspension that somehow furnished both 1g grip and a compliant ride.

"The F355 is simply the best Ferrari ever in its balance of performance, fun driving and price," asserted Luca Cifferi in *AutoWeek*. *Car and Driver* called it "Maranello's best-ever all-around sports car. No bull."

Launching the Spider version in 1995 gave Ferrari the world's first mid-engine convertible with a power-operated top. Like the GTB/GTS, it had a steel-tube chassis under a steel and aluminum body. Adroitly applied structural stiffening preserved the great suspension's stable platform, the powerful engine shrugged off the additional 100 lbs of curb weight, and lucky drivers got the sun and the moon and a real Ferrari.

Auto writer George Kacher tried one in the car's homeland, and relished "circling the Colosseum in Rome with the top down . . . trumpeting through the tunnels along northwestern Italy's Ligurian Riviera in third gear approaching 8500 rpm . . . sliding through one hairpin curve after another. . . . Even in a job rich with highlights like ours," said Kacher, "this 1100-mile trip in the droptop F355 stands out of the memory file. . . ."

Ferrari F355 Spider
1995–

Wheelbase, in. 95.6

Weight, lbs. 3250

Price $138,000

Engine dohc V-8

Displacement liters/cu. in. 3.5/213

Fuel system Fuel injection

Horsepower @ rpm 375 @ 8500

Torque @ rpm 268 @ 6000

Transmission 6-speed manual

Performance

0–60 mph, sec. 5.3

Top speed, mph 175

Almost forgotten amid the howling F50 and Ferrari's new front-engine grand touring cars is the F355. It shouldn't be. Respected voices say it may be the best all-around Ferrari sports car ever. Elements traced to the mid-1970s 308 are evident in the overall shape, transverse midships V-8 layout, and in details such as the bodyside vents. But the suspension has been honed to furnish excellent handling and an absorbent ride. The exquisite 3.5-liter twin-cam engine has five valves per cylinder and makes more than 100 hp per liter, an unprecedented specific output for a naturally aspirated V-8. The six-speed transmission works through Ferrari's trademark slotted gate. The F355 is available as the GTB coupe, GTS targa, and the captivating Spider convertible.

FIAT 124 SPORT SPIDER

A few sports cars, the Alfa Romeo Duetto for example, are fully appreciated only after they're gone. Some—most any Porsche—win accolades the moment they appear. Still others seem well regarded while in production, then their reputation fades.

Perhaps it's the Fiat lineage that tarnished the 124 Sport Spider's legacy. Possibly it's that the car wasn't very fast. Maybe its econo-sedan roots and friendly price painted a pedestrian image. But as its two-decade run unfolded, the Fiat 124 Sport Spider came to be considered an eminently enjoyable example of a fading golden age.

"It's a highly refined sports car with appealing styling, excellent ride and handling, and rather modest all-out performance," said *Road & Track* in 1976. "It isn't as new as tomorrow by any means but it has survived the test of the years to become a classic in its own time."

As with many a sports car, beneath the Spider could be found a sedan; in this case, Fiat's little 124 four-door. Starting in 1968, the Italian giant actually based two sporting cars on this platform: an airy four-passenger coupe with the standard 95.3-inch wheelbase and the Spider on a 5.5-inch shorter span. For the sporting applications, the basic 124 chassis was altered only with higher spring rates, wider tracks and wheels, and all disc instead of disc/drum brakes.

Pininfarina did the styling and the Spider never really looked out-dated, even integrating 1970s federal "crash bumpers" without much disruption. The arms-out driving position was too Italian for most, and despite a padded "back seat," this ragtop was a 2+2 in theory only. But the five-speed gearbox shifted crisply, instrumentation was thorough, and no sports car had a soft top that folded easier or sealed better.

The 96-hp 1.5-liter enlargement of the 124 engine boasted a new twincam head with toothed-belt cam drive, a world first. Displacement and tuning fluctuated during the '70s to meet U.S. smog rules. The car reached its ultimate form by 1981 as the Spider 2000, with a fuel-injected 102-hp 2.0-liter. Fiat fled the American market in 1984, but transferred Spider production and marketing to the coachbuilder, which sold an upgraded edition, the Pininfarina Azzurra, for another year or so in the United States.

Greatness doesn't require a sports car to gain stature after it retires. That it was great in its own time, on its own terms, is quite enough.

It never led its class in power or speed, but the 124 Spider was good enough to outlive most of its rivals. Fiat based it on a sedan chassis modified with a stiffer suspension and all-disc brakes. The body was a Pininfarina piece that didn't grow outdated. The smooth twincam four-cylinder engine pioneered toothed-belt cam drive, but never made much torque. Still, the steering, roadholding, and ride didn't disappoint, and the cabin was comfortable despite the arms-out driving position. Road & Track admitted being surprised when its 1970 comparison test declared the 124 Spider a more enjoyable all-around sports car than a Porsche 914, Triumph TR6, and MGB Mark 2. This Fiat always seemed to be underrated. The example pictured is a 1974 model.

Fiat 124 Sport Spider 1968–1985

Wheelbase, in. 89.7

Weight, lbs. 2500

Price $5100

Engine dohc I-4

Displacement liters/cu. in. 1.8/107

Fuel system 1 x 2 bbl. carburetor

Horsepower @ rpm 92 @ 6200

Torque @ rpm 92 @ 3000

Transmission 5-speed manual

Performance

0–60 mph, sec. 13.2

Top speed, mph 95

FORD GT40

*S*ports cars in the dual-purpose tradition began to disappear in the 1960s, as big money and advancing technology bred specialized competition machines for winning on Sunday but not necessarily going to work on Monday. Still, a few people longed for race cars that were at least semiusable on public roads, and makers such as Ferrari and Porsche occasionally obliged with low-volume "showroom" versions of various track stars.

Ford's mid-engine GT40 appeared in 1963 looking every inch the roadable racer, but it was the '66 LeMans-winning Mark II version that sired the first street edition, starting in January 1966. At a lofty $15,400, these were basically "carpeted" racers, with righthand drive and rectangular headlights, and Ford's 335-hp 289 V-8 instead of the big 485-hp 427 that finally beat Ferrari that year at LeMans.

The Mark III was announced in early 1967, just before Ford's second LeMans win with the all-American Mark IV. Though built in England like the Mark II, the III was a more practical "consumer race car," with lefthand drive, a nine-inch longer tail for six cubic feet of lug-gage space (versus none), a new nose with round sealed-beams at regulation height, and a better-appointed cockpit. The 289 returned, but at 306 hp as in Carroll Shelby's GT-350 Mustangs. Naturally, the III inherited the strong, light Mark II main structure of welded-up sheet steel, but its track was narrower and the coil/wishbone suspension was retuned for ride comfort.

For all these changes, the Mark III was far more racing fantasy than realistic road car. Though handling was competition-perfect, *Car and Driver* found acceleration only equalled that of typical Detroit muscle car: 13.8 seconds at 105 mph in the quarter-mile. Worse, workmanship was "unpardonable" for the $18,500 price, and the cockpit was a cramped, earsplitting sweatbox despite flow-through ventilation and added sound insulation. Still, said *Car and Driver*, "lay the Mk. III into a turn or see a bystander turn green with envy, and everything's almost okay again."

Of 111 original small-block GT40s, only seven were roadgoing Mark IIIs, so the hardships—and joys—of driving this beautiful and historic half-tamed racer are known to a very privileged few.

Ford GT40 Mark III
1967–1968

Wheelbase, in. 95.3

Weight, lbs. 2340

Price $18,500

Engine ohv V-8

Displacement liters/cu. in. 4.7/289

Fuel system 1 x 4 bbl. carburetor

Horsepower @ rpm 306 @ 6000

Torque @ rpm 329 @ 4200

Transmission 5-speed manual

Performance

0–60 mph, sec. 5.1

Top speed, mph 136

It was designed purely as an endurance racer, but endures as a sports car of carnal beauty. The Ford GT40 won LeMans four years running (1966–69) and dominated Sebring, Daytona, and other tracks to snare the World Sports Car Championship. The GT40—named for its 40-inch height—was built in England. Most used racing versions of Ford's 289- and 302-cid V-8s. Two LeMans winners had 427-cid V-8s, but all conformed to sports-racing rules by featuring seating for two. In all, 107 GT40s were built in a full 11 varieties. Just seven cars were intended for road use. They used detuned 289s and were designated Mark III. The GT40 pictured here is outfitted for the highway, but is a Mark II powered by a 444-hp 302 V-8 with Gurney-Weslake heads and four Weber carbs. The Mark II has a slightly shorter tail than the Mark III.

JAGUAR XK 120

*I*t's no exaggeration to say the Jaguar XK 120 helped rejuvenate a nation's belief in itself. Its seductive shape and magnificent engine brought acclaim—and orders—from all continents, reassuring Britons that their beleaguered island still could produce something of international value after World War II's devastation.

They had William Lyons to thank. Untrained as an engineer or designer, he had what proved an unerring instinct for automotive style and value. A motorcycle enthusiast as a young man, Lyons cofounded the Swallow Sidecar Company in 1921, then moved into automobiles by designing sporty bodies for other maker's chassis. His breakthrough was the splendid SS 100 (SS for Swallow Sidecar) sports car of 1936. It wasn't until after the war that his cars got their own engine, however: a 3.4-liter inline-six with an exotic-for-the-day twincam head and hemispherical combustion chambers. The work of Lyons's chief engineer, William Heynes, this engine would be Jaguar's soul into the 1980s. The six was strong and durable because it was intended for use in a sedan due in 1950. But Lyons

knew there was greater publicity value in putting it in a new sports car.

Lyons always said he drew the XK 120 with a few quick strokes of the pen, although its basic shape could be seen in an experimental stream-lined body he had done for the SS 100 in 1938. Regardless, the XK 120 was a masterwork, a low-slung roadster with pouncing-cat fender lines of disarming grace. Its underpinnings were less exciting: a shortened version of the heavy sedan chassis, independent torsion-bar front suspension, live rear axle, recirculating-ball steering, and drum brakes. No matter. Unveiled late in 1948, the car was an immediate sensation, especially at a price of around $3000.

Brakes, handling, and engine cooling could have been better, but the XK 120 was comfortable, tractable, and fast—top speed of 120 mph (hence the car's name). Early roadster bodies were aluminum, the convertible and coupe that followed were steel, while optional pistons and cams could boost horsepower to 190. In any form, the XK 120 had character and sex appeal and a significance rarely associated with automobiles.

A seminal sports car for both Jaguar and Britain was the XK 120. It used a sedan chassis and a torquey new twin-cam six that proved an instant classic. Performance rivaled cars costing much more, and though not designed for competition, the XK 120 was a race winner. The feline grace of its body was the final, magic ingredient. This is a roadster. Jaguar also built XK 120 coupes and convertibles. Total production was 12,078.

Jaguar XK 120
1948–1954

Wheelbase, in. 102.0

Weight, lbs. 2900

Price $3000

Engine dohc I-6

Displacement liters/cu. in. 3.4/210

Fuel system 2 x 1 bbl. carburetors

Horsepower @ rpm 160 @ 5000

Torque @ rpm 195 @ 2500

Transmission 4-speed manual

Performance

0–60 mph, sec. 10.0

Top speed, mph 124

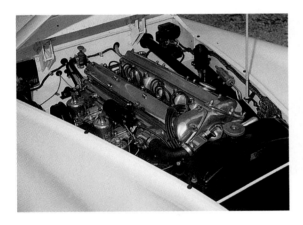

JAGUAR XK 140

So advanced and successful was the XK 120 that Jaguar didn't need to replace it for a full six years. This allowed the factory to get heavily involved in motorsports, producing the LeMans-winning C-type in 1951 and the wind-cheating D-type three years later.

Predictably, the successor XK 140 was an improved variation of the XK 120. As before, the roadster came with traditional British side curtains, the coupe and convertible with proper rollup door glass. Jaguar moved the engine/gearbox assembly forward three inches, enlarged the cockpit, and raised the rooflines slightly. That created enough room to permit a pair of very small "+2" rear seats in the coupe and convertible. It also resulted in a forward weight shift, which along with adoption of rack-and-pinion steering, improved the handling. Engine cooling was better thanks to wider-spaced grille bars.

Standard horsepower increased by 30 to 190, same as the previous $800 "special equipment" package. An "M" package added wire wheels and fog lamps, while a new "C" option brought LeMans-proven C-type cylinder heads, which were painted red and gave the 3.4 -liter

inline-six one horsepower for each of its 210 cubic inches.

On average, the 140s were about 200 lbs heavier than the 120s, and top speed didn't really increase. But John Bolster, technical editor of Britain's *Autosport*, said the 140 was "a great improvement in every important respect" over the 120. His MC coupe, heaviest of all 140s, took two gear changes and 10 seconds to reach 60 mph, but its real appeal was an ability to get to 100 mph quickly and cruise there "with only a whiff of throttle." The 140, Bolster asserted, was "the most effortless car imaginable."

In June 1955, *Road & Track* tested a $3745 MC roadster—the lightest XK 140—and saw 0–60 mph in 8.4 seconds. That, it said, was "performance per dollar excelled by no other car . . ."

These were sports-car fellows and this was sports-car nirvana. There were things Detroit still didn't seem to understand.

"The quality of finish is immediately apparent on the outside," *R&T* said of its Jaguar, "but a look under the hood shows attention to detail that is in marked contrast to that found under a domestic product."

**Jaguar XK 140
1954–1957**

Wheelbase, in. 102.0

Weight, lbs. 3150

Price $3700

Engine dohc inline-6

Displacement liters/cu. in. 3.4/210

Fuel system 2 x 1 bbl. carburetors

Horsepower @ rpm 210 @ 5750

Torque @ rpm 213 @ 4000

Transmission 4-speed manual

Performance

0–60 mph, sec. 8.4

Top speed, mph 121

Given the success of the XK 120, Jaguar made only considered changes to its successor—and took pains to retain the overall styling. For the XK 140, the engine and gearbox were moved forward and rooflines raised, creating a better-balanced sports car with a roomier cabin. The twincam six was back, but with more power. "Drop Head Coupe" is British for convertible and the one pictured has the optional M and C packages, which included wire wheels, fog lamps, and red-painted cylinder heads that gave the 3.4 liter 210 hp. Total XK 140 production was 8884; 38 percent were roadsters and the balance was split evenly between Fixed Head and Drop Head coupes.

JAGUAR XK-SS

*I*f the XK 120 rejuvenated Britain's confidence, the LeMans winners it spawned restored the country's spirit. Creating a "super sports" highway car from a LeMans victor was a fine idea—or so it must have seemed.

Jaguar tried it with the XK-SS, a high-performance roadster with roots in the world's most prestigious sports-car race. Throughout the 1950s little Jaguar battled mighty Ferrari, Maserati, and Mercedes-Benz factory teams in races heavy with nationalistic emotion. The greatest single test was LeMans, and Jaguar conquered it for England a remarkable five times.

It won in 1951 and 1953 with the XK 120C (for "competition"). These were XK 120s with space-frame chassis, redesigned suspension, and aero bodywork. The fastest got 220 hp from the twincam 3.4 six and outbraked rivals on terrific four-wheel discs. Next came the lighter, slipperier D-type, a beautiful sports-racer that won in '55, '56, and '57. With its 3.4 enlarged to 3.8 liters and 306 hp, the '57 winner hit 179 mph.

To wring some added value from the D-type at the end of its reign, Jaguar converted some into road-legal sports cars called the XK-SS. It shaved off the driver's headrest fairing, widened the monocoque, added some upholstery, a passenger-side door, a folding top with detachable side screens, and flimsy little bumpers. The only place for a muffler was on the left rocker panel, and the only place for luggage was on a decklid rack. Retained was the 44-gallon rubber-cell racing fuel tank and the dry-sump competition 3.4-liter engine.

The XK-SS was ferociously fast, stopped on a sixpence, and had a remarkably comfortable ride. But it also was cramped and noisy, and the exhaust heated up the aluminum bodywork. Racing cams concentrated power in the upper rev range, making every drive an all-out affair. Reviews were mixed. Was the XK-SS too untamed to succeed? We'll never know. On February 12, 1957, three weeks after the car's introduction, the part of the factory where it was built caught fire, destroying tooling, jigs, and partially completed cars. Jaguar was out of the super sports business, but the idea of a sports car built along D-type lines was worth pursuing. Jaguar would, and in the process create its most famous automobile.

**Jaguar XK-SS
1957**

Wheelbase, in. 90.0

Weight, lbs. NA

Price $7000

Engine dohc inline-6

Displacement liters/cu. in. 3.4/210

Fuel system 3 x 2 bbl. carburetors

Horsepower @ rpm 250 @ 5750

Torque @ rpm 242 @ 4000

Transmission 4-speed manual

Performance

0–60 mph, sec. 5.6

Top speed, mph 149

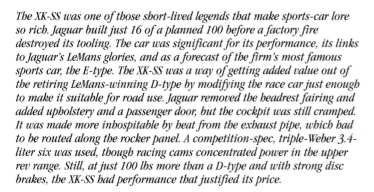

*The XK-SS was one of those short-lived legends that make sports-car lore
so rich. Jaguar built just 16 of a planned 100 before a factory fire
destroyed its tooling. The car was significant for its performance, its links
to Jaguar's LeMans glories, and as a forecast of the firm's most famous
sports car, the E-type. The XK-SS was a way of getting added value out of
the retiring LeMans-winning D-type by modifying the race car just enough
to make it suitable for road use. Jaguar removed the headrest fairing and
added upholstery and a passenger door, but the cockpit was still cramped.
It was made more inhospitable by heat from the exhaust pipe, which had
to be routed along the rocker panel. A competition-spec, triple-Weber 3.4-
liter six was used, though racing cams concentrated power in the upper
rev range. Still, at just 100 lbs more than a D-type and with strong disc
brakes, the XK-SS had performance that justified its price.*

JAGUAR XK 150

Some say the XK 150 proves that Jaguar's first postwar sports cars hung on too long. They may be right, but the 150 was also the most thoroughly developed of the early XKs, if arguably the least sporting. This final variation on the original XK 120 theme was Jaguar's response to recently introduced rivals such as the BMW 507 and Mercedes-Benz 300SL, which bettered the XK 140 in catering to American demands for more comfort and refinement.

The 150 was thus roomier, plusher, and more civilized than any previous XK. And the bodyshell was restyled, losing some pouncing-cat contours and gaining a wider grille and one-piece windshield. Critics bemoaned the heavier appearance, especially since it was matched by higher curb weight. Fortunately, the extra heft didn't spoil overall handling balance. And Jaguar scored a production first by replacing fade-prone drum brakes with four servo-assisted Dunlop discs that easily compensated for the extra weight. The discs had demonstrated their value on Jaguar's LeMans winners.

Initially, the XK 150 was offered as a coupe and convertible. The roadster returned after nine months, but now with wind-up windows. Engine specs were the same as the 140, but the 150's extra weight prompted more buyers to pop for the 210-hp option, which now produced peak torque at 3000 rpm, not 4000. Not coincidentally, the extra-cost automatic transmission also garnered more orders, a sure sign of change in the sports-car world.

Inevitably, the first XK 150s were slower than their predecessors, but the deficit was corrected in the spring of 1958 with a 3.4-liter "S" engine rated at 250 hp. For 1960, Jaguar bored its 3.4 to 3.8 liters, rating this option at 220 hp in standard tune or 265 in "S" form. A 3.8-liter 150S could top 135 mph and sprint from 0–60 mph in around 7.0 seconds, thus restoring whatever verve the XK had been missing.

Though not the longest-lived, the 150 proved the most profitable of the original XK series. Tellingly, where roadsters had been the best-selling XK 120 and 140 body styles, the coupe was by far the most popular 150, accounting for 52 percent of sales. The roadster was the least popular, at just 13 percent. William Lyons had correctly read the evolving market and, with the XK 150's successor, he'd do it again.

Jaguar XK 150
1957–1960

Wheelbase, in. 102.0

Weight, lbs. 3500

Price $4800

Engine dohc inline-6

Displacement liters/cu. in. 3.4/210

Fuel system 2 x 1 bbl. carburetors

Horsepower @ rpm 190 @ 5500

Torque @ rpm 210 @ 2500

Transmission 4-speed manual

Performance

0–60 mph, sec. 11.5

Top speed, mph 120

Jaguar's final XK 120 variation was the XK 150. It bowed in 1957 as a revamp of the XK 140. Its styling was stodgier, it was heavier, and at first it had no more power. But it was among the first cars with standard four-wheel disc brakes. Fewer buyers ordered manual transmission, but those who did could activate overdrive with a floor lever rather than a dashboard toggle (above right). With 9395 built, the XK 150 outsold the XK 140. The most popular body style was the coupe. This one has the base 190-hp 3.4-liter six. A LeMans lineage still mattered, as evidenced by the XK 150's badge (bottom left).

JAGUAR E-TYPE

*I*n the world of '60s sports cars, this is where sex appeal came for lessons. Ferraris were provocative. Jaguar's E-type—XK-E in America—was positively suggestive. An awed *Road & Track* subtitled its test report, "The greatest crumpet collector known to man."

Of course there was far more to it than libidinal lines. Its performance was predatory. Jaguar took the hot S-spec 3.8 from the XK 150 and moved the big inline-six rearward to redistribute weight 49/51. The new car was shorter and lighter than its predecessor, and added a vital component even the LeMans winners lacked: independent rear suspension. Construction, too, improved on the racing D-type's, with a monocoque (unitized) bodyshell in a choice of roadster or new hatchback coupe. Styling was by aerodynamicist Malcolm Sayer, making this the first production Jaguar not shaped by William Lyons. Still, the founder's hand was evident in the overall character of the car, as well as in its well-appointed, if cozy, cabin and in its reasonable price.

Jaguar unveiled its E-type in March 1961 at the same Geneva show that launched the XK 120 13 years before, and to the same frenzied reception.

"Here we have one of the quietest and most flexible cars on the market, capable of whispering along in top gear at 10 mph or leaping into its 150 mph stride on the brief depression of a pedal," wrote John Bolster of *Autosport*. The new all-independent suspension provided a comfortable ride and combined four-wheel discs (inboard in back) for outstanding all-around road manners. There even was decent luggage space.

The E-type of 1965 got a displacement increase to 4.2 liters for better torque but no more horsepower. The following year brought a 2+2 coupe with a nine-inch-longer wheelbase, taller roofline, and optional automatic transmission. Styling of Series 2 models suffered in the late '60s from side marker lights, clumsier bumpers, and upright exposed headlamps. But that hardly dulled their appeal. The E-type helped define the 1960s and to this day is one of the precious few sports cars to command the attention even of people who care little about automobiles.

Jaguar E-type
1961–1964

Wheelbase, in. 96.0

Weight, lbs. 2720

Price $5595

Engine dohc I-6

Displacement liters/cu. in. 3.8/231

Fuel system 3 x 1 bbl. carburetors

Horsepower @ rpm 265 @ 5500

Torque @ rpm 260 @ 4000

Transmission 4-speed manual

Performance

0–60 mph, sec. 6.9

Top speed, mph 153

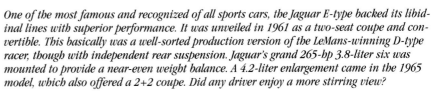

One of the most famous and recognized of all sports cars, the Jaguar E-type backed its libidinal lines with superior performance. It was unveiled in 1961 as a two-seat coupe and convertible. This basically was a well-sorted production version of the LeMans-winning D-type racer, though with independent rear suspension. Jaguar's grand 265-hp 3.8-liter six was mounted to provide a near-even weight balance. A 4.2-liter enlargement came in the 1965 model, which also offered a 2+2 coupe. Did any driver enjoy a more stirring view?

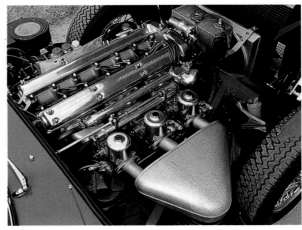

JAGUAR E-TYPE SERIES 3 V-12

*I*t was a smashing success once, in 1948, when Jaguar debuted its robust new engine in a sports car instead of the sedan for which it was designed. But the inline-six that met its public in the XK 120 was 23 years old by 1971, and enfeebled by emissions regulations. The E-type was 10 years old and needed new life. Why not put the new passenger-car V-12 in a revised version of the aging sports model?

Despite its sports-car heritage, Jaguar depended on sedans for its survival and had developed its twelve to power them with sufficient torque and refinement. It was beefy enough to handle up to 7.0 liters displacement, but an initial volume of 5.3 was chosen. The all-aluminum single-cam V-12 was about three inches longer than the inline-six, and though it outweighed the six by less than 75 lbs, it still tipped the scales at almost 700 lbs. Jaguar rated it at 272 hp in Europe and 314 in the United States, though a realistic American figure was 250 hp at 6000 rpm and 283 lb/ft of torque at 3500. Installed in the E-type, it created the Series 3.

The new engine fit in the same bay as the six, but for better leg room

Jaguar shelved the convertible's 96-inch wheelbase and gave all Series 3s the 105-inch span previously exclusive to the 2+2 coupes. A larger radiator inlet with formal grillework and subtle wheel arches to clear wider tires were other changes. Larger, softer in nature, with weight redistributed 53/47, the E-type had lost the wilds of its youth.

"Perhaps a little naively," said Robert Bell in *Motor*, "all we expected to try was a new engine. What in fact we drove was a new car—not a yowling, aggressive Ferrari-like machine, with which, perhaps, most people associate a V12 engine, but a very smooth, quiet and refined grand touring sports car." Still, newer rivals had better ergonomics, were more reliable, and just felt more modern. "A magnificent engine in an outclassed body," was how *Road & Track* saw the Series 3.

Jaguar had not duplicated its success of 1948, and it would be years before any of its sports models generated even a flicker of that excitement. Encounter a V-12 E-type, though, and see if you don't study it long and hard.

Its classic inline six enfeebled by emissions standards, Jaguar in 1971 turned to V-12 power for the E-type. This created the Series 3, which came as a two-seat convertible or a 2+2 coupe, both on the longer of two wheelbases that had been offered on the six-cylinder E-types. The cars had lost their enchanting headlamp covers in late 1964, and the Series 3 added a larger radiator inlet screened by formal grillework and subtle wheel arches to clear wider tires. New safety rules mandated rocker switches on the still-handsome dashboard. The signature hood bulge was retained, but wasn't needed to clear the new engine. Jaguar rated the 5.3-liter twelve at 314 hp, and if the E-type was now more of a grand tourer, it was no less alluring. Jaguar built 15,290 Series 3, 18,808 Series 2, and 38,410 Series 1 roadgoing E-types.

Jaguar E-type Series 3 V-12 1971–1975

Wheelbase, in. 105.0

Weight, lbs. 3200

Price $8800

Engine ohc V-12

Displacement liters/cu. in. 5.3/326

Fuel system 4 x 1 bbl. carburetors

Horsepower @ rpm 314 @ 6200

Torque @ rpm 349 @ 6300

Transmission 4-speed manual

Performance

0–60 mph, sec. 7.2

Top speed, mph 143

JAGUAR XJ220

*W*as ever there a supercar with so grand a beginning and so ignominious an end? Jaguar's XJ220 appeared to have it all: a beautiful aluminum body, buyers queuing up with cash in hand, a 200-mph top speed. How then was it reduced to a fender-banging embarrassment in cable-TV exhibition races? And why did Jaguar end up suing some XJ220 customers?

It all started well enough, the concept XJ220 garnering raves at its 1988 unveiling. Conceived as a road car capable of racing in the Group B series that generated the Porsche 959 and Ferrari F40, the XJ220 had a 520-hp V-12, all-wheel drive, four-wheel steering, and bold jack-knife doors. By December 1990, Jaguar had set a price of $536,000 and quickly collected 1500 deposits of $92,500 each; it returned all but 350—the number of XJ220s it planned to build. Group B dried up, but the XJ220 survived in what Jaguar believed was a more marketable form.

The production XJ220 completed in June 1992 was a two-seat mid-

engine coupe visually similar to the original. But it had a 542-hp 3.5-liter twin-turbo V-6, rear-wheel drive, and conventional steering and doors. It was quiet, comfortable, and very fast; even if it didn't reach the 220-mph target that was the basis of its name, it confidently exceeded 210.

But it wasn't the V-12 techno-wonder that had been promised, and in a faltering supercar market, Jaguar could unload fewer than 170 of the 265 XJ220s it eventually built. Scores of original depositors who refused to take delivery were sued for not honoring their contracts.

To promote the car, Jaguar and the ESPN sports network cooked up Fast Masters, in which retired race drivers ran XJ220s at tiny Indianapolis Raceway Park. The long-legged exotics were out of their element. *AutoWeek*'s Denise McCluggage likened it to "racing thoroughbreds around the dining room table." Much lovely aluminum was rearranged. On the open road, the XJ220 delivered. It was others who broke their promises.

The XJ220 had the potential to be a highly successful supercar, but ended up an embarrassment. Jaguar unveiled the mid-engine two-seater in 1988 with a V-12, jackknife doors, and all-wheel drive and steering. When it went into production in 1992, circumstances had changed and the car had a twin-turbo V-6, rear drive, and conventional doors. It was very fast and very beautiful, but some customers who had put down their money for the exotic V-12 version refused delivery. Legal entanglements followed, and at one point, Jaguar raced the sleek supercar in a fender-smashing short-track series for cable TV.

Jaguar XJ220
1992–1993

Wheelbase, in. 104.0

Weight, lbs. 3025

Price $536,000

Engine Twin turbo dohc V-12

Displacement liters/cu. in. 3.5/215

Fuel system Fuel injection

Horsepower @ rpm 542 @ 7000

Torque @ rpm 475 @ 4500

Transmission 5-speed manual

Performance

0–60 mph, sec. 4.8

Top speed, mph 210

JAGUAR XK8

New Jaguars don't appear that often, so the 1996 arrival of the XK8 was a big event. Not only the first clean-sheet Jaguar since 1987's "XJ40" sedans, it's the first with a V-8—itself only the fourth major engine in Jaguar history. Moreover, this new coupe and convertible are the first XK Jaguars since the beloved E-type (a.k.a. XK-E) died 21 years before.

Yet despite its wonderfully evocative styling, the XK8 does not pick up where the E-type left off. Jaguar may call it a sports car, but it's really a posh grand tourer like the model it replaces, the XJS. Indeed, the XK8 uses part of the S-type platform, rides the same classic, all-independent double-wishbone suspension, and offers similarly luxurious "2+2" accommodations.

The XJS was hooted on its 1975 debut for abandoning sports-car basics as much as for its controversial coupe styling. But Jaguar knew what people wanted. With steady improvements to its big V-12, and the later addition of convertible and six-cylinder models, the S actually gained in annual sales as time passed.

It was thus logical that the XK8 would follow a similar formula. The XK8 originated soon after Ford bought Jaguar in 1990 and axed an erstwhile

E-type successor dubbed XK-F (some of which was later salvaged for the Aston Martin DB7). Meanwhile, Jaguar was investigating V-8s and had a prototype engine running by late 1991. Two years after that, Ford approved a V-8 XJS replacement coded "X100," and the XK8 was a showroom reality just 30 months later. That was warp-speed for tiny Jaguar, but the X100 team received valuable timesaving pointers from the Ford crew working on the new '94 Mustang.

The result blends traditional Jaguar elegance with American manufacturing professionalism. XK8 not only is rock-solid and free of quirky details, it's agile like the XJS never was. It's fast, too, thanks to that muscular new "AJ-V8." An all-Jaguar, all-alloy, twincam engine (what else from Coventry?), the AJ-V8 relishes revs, yet never rises above a muted growl. And it mates beautifully with a new five-speed automatic transmission from Germany's ZF that changes gears like a mercury switch.

A pure sports car? No, the XK8 is far too refined for that, but it is a genuine sporting Jaguar and modern in every way. If that's not something to celebrate, nothing is.

Jaguar XK8
1996–

Wheelbase, in. 101.9

Weight, lbs. 3867

Price $69,900

Engine dohc V-8

Displacement liters/cu. in. 4.0/244

Fuel system Fuel injection

Horsepower @ rpm 290 @ 6100

Torque @ rpm 290 @ 4200

Transmission 5-speed manual

Performance

0–60 mph, sec. 6.7

Top speed, mph 154

The XK8 puts Jaguar's sports-car credentials in order for the first time since the E-type. It comes as a coupe and convertible and features Jaguar's first V-8 engine.

JENSEN-HEALEY

*R*ecapturing past glories can be a tricky business. Take the Jensen-Healey. *Road & Track* concluded its 1973 test of the car with this lament: "To remember the originality, the impact, the appeal of the original Austin-Healey is to know and regret that the Jensen-Healey is only competitive with cars in its class."

The Jensen and Healey names first linked in the mid 1950s, when British Motor Corporation tapped specialty builder Jensen to supply Austin-Healey bodies. Jensen was selling its own cars by then—fast grand touring coupes built in small numbers with Chrysler V-8 power. But body and assembly contracts remained one of its major revenue sources into the late '60s. Then the contracts dried up, car sales weakened, and Jensen was on the financial ropes.

Enter Kjell Qvale, veteran San Francisco import-car baron and U.S. Jensen distributor. Qvale had sold a lot of Austin-Healeys, and thought a modern successor would do well enough to turn Jensen around. With this as the core of a rescue package, Qvale bought the firm while persuading Donald Healey and son Geoff to lend their talents—and name—to a new

moderately priced open two-seater—a "Big Healey" for the '70s.

Unfortunately, the convertible that arrived in 1972 was far less memorable than the late Austin-Healey. Styling was unexceptional, steering and coil-spring live-rear-axle suspension were Vauxhall (British GM) parts, and the four-speed gearbox came from Chrysler UK. Though it was based on a production Vauxhall unit, at least the engine was advanced: a new 2.0-liter 16-valve twin-cam four-cylinder built by Lotus.

Despite its mixed parentage, the J-H offered fine handling and good performance even in smog-legal U.S. tune. But cowl shake and a clumsy top did not appeal, bodies rusted ferociously, and the Lotus engine was less than reliable.

With all this, sales ran well below expectations, and there was no help from a five-speed gearbox (for '73) nor a posh, squarish GT coupe companion (announced in mid 1975). The venture finally folded in 1976. Faults notwithstanding, the Jensen-Healey was a credible old-school sports car. But it wasn't superior to rivals from bigger, more established companies, and it was certainly no Austin-Healey.

Jensen-Healey
1972–1976

Wheelbase, in. 92.0

Weight, lbs. 2155

Price $5000

Engine dohc I-4

Displacement liters/cu. in. 2.0/121

Fuel system 2 x 1 bbl. carburetors

Horsepower @ rpm 140 @ 6500

Torque @ rpm 130 @ 5000

Transmission 5-speed manual

Performance

0–60 mph, sec. 9.7

Top speed, mph 120

Speciality builder Jensen linked with sports-car legend Healey in the early 1970s to build what should have been a successful new roadster. But problems were afoot, starting with the uninspired styling. Rather ordinary passenger-car suspension pieces gave responsive handling, and all-around performance was good. But the Lotus-built twincam four was trouble prone, the body panels rusted, and the cowl shook badly over rough pavement. Competitive pricing helped sell 10,926 Jensen-Healeys, but the car did nothing for the reputation of either name.

LAMBORGHINI MIURA

*G*reat sports cars are enveloped by legend, and so it is with the Miura, the world's first mid-engine supercar, a sensuous wonder whose daring design embarrassed even Ferrari.

Ferruccio Lamborghini's plunge into the auto business is itself the material of myth. Born to farmers, he was a self-made industrialist (tractors, heating systems), and a lover of fast cars. It's said that when Enzo Ferrari refused to personally attend to his complaint about a sick Ferrari, the ego-charged Ferruccio vowed to create his own exotic. That first Lamborghini, built from 1964 to '68, was a front-engine V-12 coupe, a comfortable swift *gran turismo* that suited Ferruccio's middle-age style. When his talented engineers, led by 24-year-old Giampaolo Dallara, got Lamborghini to OK something racier, the result stole the show at the 1965 Turin exhibition. It was just a bare chassis, but was so spectacular in its racing-derived layout and so breathtaking in its use of a transverse-mounted V-12 engine, that tradition says a beaming Ferruccio collected deposits from buyers who didn't know the machine had no body and no name.

Enter Marcello Gandini, 25, a brilliant Bertone stylist who fashioned a lean, low two-seater—a young-man's exotic—that blew the lid off the '66 Geneva show. It was designated P400: P for *posteriore*, or aft-mounted engine, and 400 in reference to the V-12's displacement. Lamborghini, however, looked to his Taurus birth sign and to the ferocious fighting bulls of Don Eduardo Miura and christened the thing Miura (MYUR-ah).

This was no GT in the original Lamborghini mold, but a cramped, fatiguing, poor-shifting, hothouse of a 350-hp supercar. Yet its enthralling acceleration, race-worthy cornering, howling top speed, and of course its styling, overwhelmed everything. Many flaws, including the most serious—nose lift at high speed—diminished as the Miura evolved through the 370-hp P400S of 1969 to the 385-hp SV of 1971. That last was the best. It wisely retained the look of the original and, like every Miura, was legend made real.

Lamborghini Miura SV
1971–1972

Wheelbase, in. 97.75

Weight, lbs. 2737

Price $20,500

Engine dohc V-12

Displacement liters/cu. in. 3.9/240

Fuel system 4 x 2 bbl. carburetors

Horsepower @ rpm 385 @ 7850

Torque @ rpm 294 @ 5750

Transmission 5-speed manual

Performance

0–60 mph, sec. 5.5

Top speed, mph 168

Lamborghini invented the modern supercar with the Miura. It debuted twice, first in 1965 as a bare chassis that sent rich enthusiasts for their wallets, then in 1966 with a body by Bertone stylist Marcello Gandini that electrified the motoring world. By setting its howling V-12 midships and transversely, the Miura was the first production car to use racetrack technology for strictly highway purposes. Gandini was inspired by the look and design of the Ford GT40, and mimicked the racer by using a steel central body as part of the structure, then mounting aluminum nose and tail sections as unstressed units that hinged open. Putting the engine sideways allowed the seats to be set well behind the front wheels and comfortably apart. The cabin was still a hot, noisy place, but with the potential to exceed 160 mph, some compromises were necessary. Front-end lift was a problem at those speeds, and handling was not for the faint of heart. The twincam V-12 stayed at 3.9 liters, but rose from 350 hp to 370 and finally to 385 in the SV version (pictured).

LAMBORGHINI COUNTACH

*F*ortunate is the automaker that fields one unprecedented design; at the 1971 Geneva motor show, tiny Lamborghini unveiled its second. The Miura's successor had science-fiction looks and otherworldly performance. By the time it went into production in 1974, motoring's outer limits had a new address: Countach.

Its wheelbase was shorter than the Miura's and instead of a unitized central steel shell, Countach had a welded-tube chassis supporting a non-stressed aluminum skin. Styling was again the work of Marcello Gandini, but where his Miura was all luscious curves, this new car took the wedge profile to its extreme. Asymmetric rear-wheel arches, "scissor" opening doors, and immodest vents and scoops iced the fearless package. "The Countach," said Britain's *Car* magazine, "breathes naked aggression from every pore."

In practice, the shovel nose killed any hint of high-speed lift, and the scoops fed radiators logically located in the rear flanks. The Miura's transverse V-12 was cleverly rotated to face rearward. This put the shift linkage under the driver's hand for smoother action and rearranging the drivetrain mass for safer cornering and better containment of heat and noise. The Countach (COON-tahsh) was even quicker and handled better than the

Miura, but it was an automobile that demanded real commitment.

Lifting the doors was a chore, and getting in or out required sliding over broad sills that harbored the fuel tanks. Footwells were narrow and angled, the windscreen acted as a greenhouse, only part of the side glass opened, and visibility was awful. But few contemporaries were as fast, and none was as wanton. This car, wrote journalist Pete Lyons, "treats velocity with the same casual contempt it does society."

The original Countach LP 400 was followed by the LP 400 S (235 built, 1978–82), which added fiberglass wheelarches and fatter tires. The V-12 grew to 4.8 liters for the LP 5000 S (323 built, 1982–85); it had the same 375 hp as the first two versions but more torque. The LP 5000 QV (610 built, 1985–88) had 5.2 liters and up to 455 hp from *Quattrovalvole*, or four-valve, heads. Fuel injection in '86 made the Countach U.S. smog-legal for the first time since the '70s, but the car carried ugly federal bumpers. Chrysler bought Lamborghini from interim Swiss owners in 1987 and oversaw the release of the final Countach, the 455-hp Anniversary Edition. With 650 built from 1988 to 90, this was the most popular, most refined, and possibly the fastest Countach: 0–60 mph in 4.7 seconds and 183 mph all out.

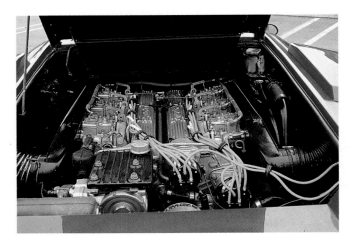

Lamborghini's follow-up to the Miura took the mid-engine supercar to its carnivorous extreme. It was called Countach, an Italian slang that roughly translates to "That's it." Its maker saw the car as a low-volume image builder. It turned out to be Lamborghini's biggest seller ever. Fender flares and spoilers were added over the years, but this original LP 400 shows the stunning core shape was present from the start. Among the constants were scissor-opening doors, a hard-to-negotiate interior, and a midships V-12. This 3.9-liter has 24 valves and 375 hp. Ultimate versions had 5.2 liters, 48 valves, and 455 hp.

Lamborghini Countach LP 400
1974–1978

Wheelbase, in. 95.5

Weight, lbs. 2860

Price $45,000

Engine dohc V-12

Displacement liters/cu. in. 3.9/240

Fuel system 6 x 2 bbl. carburetors

Horsepower @ rpm 375 @ 8000

Torque @ rpm 286 @ 5000

Transmission 5-speed manual

Performance

0–60 mph, sec. 5.6

Top speed, mph 179

LAMBORGHINI DIABLO

*L*amborghini's follow-up to the Countach was a hyper exotic for a changed world. No longer could a supercar get by merely on irrational styling and unfettered performance. It had to satisfy safety and emissions standards, even offer a measure of refinement.

In balancing these demands, the Diablo came closer to fulfilling founder Ferruccio's dream of a do-everything GT than any other midships Lamborghini. That's not to suggest this car is tame. It's named, after all, for both a fighting bull and the devil himself. "In the grand and romantic tradition of the Italian Supercar," said *Motor Trend*, "the Diablo is a thundering, fuel-sucking exercise in excess."

Larger, wider, heavier, and more aerodynamic than the Countach, the Diablo's 202-mph top speed made it the planet's fastest car upon its unveiling in 1990. The basic design, by Marcello Gandini of Miura and Countach fame, retained such Countach elements as asymmetric rear-wheel cutouts and scissor doors, but had a fresh cab-forward silhouette and dramatic plunging A-pillars. This was the first Lamborghini developed under Chrysler, which furnished computer-design expertise and also softened the lines of

Gandini's original styling. The body was a new mix of steel, aluminum, and composite panels. The space-frame chassis was evolved from Countach's, but was stronger and exceeded worldwide crash standards.

Lamborghini again mounted a 48-valve V-12 longitudinally and "backward," but now it had 5.7 liters, was computer managed, and made 485 hp. Debuting in 1990 at $220,000, the Diablo was engineered from the start for four-wheel drive, and in 1993 came the 492-hp, $239,000 VT model. Its *Visco Traction* system sent 15 percent of the power to the front wheels when the rears slipped. In 1994, off came the VT hardware, plus 386 lbs of other "amenities," for the 30th Anniversary Special Edition Diablo, a $257,000, 525-hp, 206-mph demon. As an encore, Lamborghini in 1996 delivered the world's fastest four-wheel-drive convertible, the VT roadster with a removable carbon-fiber roof panel.

In 1994, Chrysler sold out to MegaTech Ltd., an Indonesian firm that seems intent on keeping Lamborghini vital. There's a planned successor to the Diablo, so the raging bull will continue aboard a mid-engine supercar, the breed Lamborghini originated and insists on perpetuating.

Lamborghini Diablo Roadster 1996–

Wheelbase, in. 106.0

Weight, lbs. 3900

Price $270,500

Engine dohc V-12

Displacement liters/cu. in. 5.7/348

Fuel system Fuel injection

Horsepower @ rpm 492 @ 7000

Torque @ rpm 428 @ 5200

Transmission 5-speed manual

Performance

0–60 mph, sec. 4.6

Top speed, mph 185

True to tradition, Lamborghini's supercar for the '90s was named for a fighting bull, but Diablo also is another word for devil. Indeed, it certainly has enough power to feel possessed. Compared to the Countach, Diablo is longer, wider, heavier, stronger, and safer. Its basic design is the work of Marcello Gandini, who also did the Miura and Countach, but Diablo came to fruition when Lamborghini was owned by Chrysler, and the American company's hand is evident in some styling touches and production techniques. The car retains the scissor doors made famous by the Countach, but also offers the convertible body style shown here. The roof panel stores above the engine hatch. Its 48-valve 5.7-liter V-12 has 492 hp, but some editions have had 525. The Roadster also employs a permanently engaged all-wheel-drive system to help keep this cocky spirit under control.

LOTUS ELAN

Colin Chapman was a canny Brit whose credo was that simplicity, lightness, and streamlining wins the race. After a modest start in the late 1940s souping-up tiny Austin Sevens, he formed Lotus Cars in 1952 and won fame with aluminum-bodied sports-racers that proved giant-killers despite small engines and somewhat fragile natures. Lotus soon expanded into road cars with the stark, speedy Seven roadster, followed in 1959 by the elegant Elite coupe, the world's first production car with fully unitized fiberglass construction.

In 1962, Chapman changed the shape of racing with rear-engine Formula 1 and Indianapolis cars. They made Lotus the decade's dominant power in international open-wheel competition. That same year brought an equally revolutionary roadgoing Lotus, the Elan. Like the Elite, it was a petite fiberglass-bodied two-seater with a front four-cylinder engine, all-disc brakes, rack-and-pinion steering, and all-coil independent suspension with rear MacPherson struts. Also per Lotus tradition, the Elan was sold in both assembled and kit form (the latter avoiding high taxes in Britain).

But the Elan was a far more practical—and saleable—Lotus than the Elite. A neatly styled roadster with hidden headlamps, it eschewed its predecessor's nervous Coventry-Climax engine for a larger, more reliable British Ford-based unit with a new Lotus-designed twincam cylinder head that gave all kinds of revvy performance in concert with Chapman's weight-conscious engineering. The Elan also pioneered a new Lotus hallmark: a sturdy sheet-steel "backbone" chassis with forked ends for carrying the drivetrain and final drive. Though the design dictated a high center tunnel, it made for flat cornering and super-responsive handling that were state-of-the-sports-car art.

The Elan evolved steadily over a dozen years, gaining a bit more power, a companion coupe, and nicer appointments, even siring a stretched "+2" coupe series. The final version, the 1971–74 Sprint, was arguably the best, thanks to its 126-hp "Big Valve" engine. Yet every Elan was what *Road & Track* once called "a gutty little car, highly refined in some areas and crude in others. [It calls] for a lot of concentration and skill if the driver is to handle it smoothly—[but] the rewards of great cornering powers and a marvelously intimate connection between driver and road are worth the trouble." Colin Chapman wouldn't have it any other way.

The Elan was the road car that successfully translated Colin Chapman's race-bred philosophy that lighter is better. It used a steel backbone chassis and a fiberglass body with then-novel hidden headlamps. A hardtop also was offered. The Lotus-made engine put a twincam head on a Ford block. The communicative Elan cornered like a go-cart and accelerated well for its modest power, but assembly quality was spotty. The steering wheel on this example is not original.

Lotus Elan
1962–1974

Wheelbase, in. 84.0

Weight, lbs. 1515

Price $4160

Engine dohc I-4

Displacement liters/cu. in. 1.6/95

Fuel system 2 x 2 bbl. carburetors

Horsepower @ rpm 105 @ 5500

Torque @ rpm 108 @ 4000

Transmission 4-speed manual

Performance

0–60 mph, sec. 9.0

Top speed, mph 115

LOTUS ESPRIT V-8

*S*ome cars get better with age. Take the Lotus Esprit. The 1996 V-8 model isn't just the newest sports car from "Britain's Porsche," it's the ultimate version of a contemporary classic, a car that's seen Lotus through good times and bad.

Entering production in 1975, the Esprit was the second roadgoing mid-engine Lotus, after the 1967-vintage Europa. In addition to the established marque hallmarks of two-seat fiberglass bodywork, steel backbone chassis, and race-proved independent suspension, the Esprit had trendy "doorstop" styling by Italy's Giorgetto Giugiaro and Lotus's new 2.0-liter twincam four. It was mounted longitudinally and delivered 160 hp (140 in U.S. tune) through a five-speed transaxle for 0–60 mph in nine seconds or less.

The 1982 death of founder Colin Chapman began a troubled era for Lotus, but the Esprit hung on as sister models died. The first major improvements came with 1980's "S2.2," named for its enlarged 2.2-liter engine. More exciting was a 150-mph Turbo Esprit with 210 hp, a stiffer chassis,

larger wheels and brakes, and revised suspension that also benefitted 1981's non-turbo Series 3. SE models debuted in 1987 with 228 hp in the Turbo, then 264 from '89, and a smooth-contour restyle by Britisher Peter Stevens. The replacement S4s of '93 were the most luxurious Esprits ever and sired the strongest of the four-cylinder breed, the turbo Sport 300 and similar S4S, both with 300 hp and sub-five-second 0–60 ability.

Despite such performance, turbo Esprits were always high-strung mounts demanding an expert driver (preferably of jockey build) and a rich man's means. Today, thanks to Lotus's new 350-hp aluminum twin-cam twin-turbo V-8, the Esprit fulfills Chapman's original vision of a smooth, refined, mid-engine supercar—though it's only about as quick as an S4S. Still, wrote Paul Frere for *Road & Track,* it "puts you in charge of a wonderful engine, performance in the Porsche Turbo class, superb handling and a surprisingly good ride." What's more, 20 years of careful honing finally produced a Lotus "that is beautifully made, down to the smallest details."

Lotus has maintained its identity as a small British boutique builder despite being owned over the years by giants such as General Motors. Its core product is the Esprit, a mid-engine exotic that dates from 1975. Like Porsche with its 911, Lotus has refined and fortified the Esprit over the decades. Building on a sound backbone chassis design and original styling by Giorgetto Giugiaro, the Esprit evolved from a naturally aspirated four-cylinder sports car with as little as 140 hp to a turbocharged one with as much as 300. The latest version wears a fetching late-1980s styling update by Britisher Peter Stevens and features the line's first V-8 engine. The 350-hp twin-turbo 3.5 (right) provides more flexible performance than the turbo fours and, combined with better-than-ever assembly quality, makes the Esprit all a bona fide supercar should be.

Lotus Esprit V-8
1996–

Wheelbase, in. 96.0

Weight, lbs. 3040

Price $85,640

Engine Twin turbo dohc V-8

Displacement liters/cu. in. 3.5/214

Fuel system Fuel injection

Horsepower @ rpm 350 @ 6500

Torque @ rpm 295 @ 4250

Transmission 5-speed manual

Performance

0–60 mph, sec. 4.5

Top speed, mph 178

MASERATI 3500GT

*B*y the late 1950s, everyone knew a sports car looked like a Jaguar XK 140 or an MGA. But there was another species, one less obviously racy, more scarce, very costly, and quite self-assured.

The Maserati brothers started building racing cars in the 1920s, and for four decades their trident was a force from the Grands Prix of Europe to the bricks of Indianapolis. In 1957, Juan Manuel Fangio won his fifth Formula 1 Championship in a Maserati. The brothers had by then sold out to deeper pockets (and continued racing by founding OSCA), but Maserati's new owners developed money problems of their own and sought a cure through "volume" production of sporting road cars.

The 3500GT was actually the third Maserati street machine; about 140 others had trickled out since World War II. But it was the first to match the benchmark Ferrari in prestige and performance, and it did so with little fanfare and no lack of confidence. *Motor Life*'s Wayne Thoms gained a new perspective driving a 3500GT coupe around Beverly Hills in 1961. "The Maser embodies the secret of a modern classic, a design so handsome, so simple, that it blends unobtrusively with whatever surrounding is at hand," he wrote. "[I]t was a pleasant thing, driving an extremely expensive, extremely rare, highly sporting machine without feeling obligated to win two or three stop light drags every mile."

Aside from the engine, little about the car was extraordinary, but the blend worked exceptionally well and was wrapped in elegant coachwork. Buyers could choose a 2+2 coupe from Touring of Milan or a convertible by Vignale of Turin on a two-inch shorter wheelbase. Both used a chassis of steel tubes and panels that was unadventuresome but sturdy. There were coil springs in front, a live axle and leaf springs in back. Front disc brakes and a limited-slip differential were options after 1958, but rack-and-pinion steering never arrived.

Underhood was the real treat: a detuned Maserati sports-racing engine. The all-aluminum twincam inline-six had hemispherical combustion chambers and twin spark plugs. It drove through a four-speed ZF gearbox, with a five speed optional from 1960 and standard from '61. The trio of Webers eventually was supplanted by Lucas mechanical fuel injection, bringing another 15 hp and a GTI badge. The 3500GT was followed by a long line of Maserati GTs, but none approached its understated self-assurance.

Maserati's first real challenge to Ferrari was the understated but highly capable 3500GT. It came as the 2+2 coupe pictured or as a two-seat convertible on a shorter wheelbase. The all-alloy twincam six was a detuned Maserati racing engine. In 1961, fuel injection replaced the three Webers shown here and brought a GTI designation. Total production of the classy GT/GTI was 2223.

Maserati 3500GT
1957–1964

Wheelbase, in. 102.2

Weight, lbs. 3180

Price $11,400

Engine dohc I-6

Displacement liters/cu. in. 3.5/213

Fuel system 3 x 2 bbl. carburetors

Horsepower @ rpm 220 @ 5500

Torque @ rpm 253 @ 3500

Transmission 5-speed manual

Performance

0–60 mph, sec. 8.1

Top speed, mph 140

MASERATI BORA

After the well-bred 3500, Maserati introduced a series of ultra-conventional GTs that, except for the Giugiaro-styled Ghibli in 1966, failed to ignite much passion. By 1970, the hottest exoticars were mid-engined, a movement Maserati finally joined in 1971 with the Bora.

This was another Giugiaro work, one *Road & Track* called "strikingly handsome, clean and slightly brutal-looking." It employed an all-steel unibody and a longitudinal drivetrain mounted to a bolted-on subframe. Separated from the two-seat cabin by double-pane rear glass and an upholstered cover was another tamed Maserati racing engine: a 310-hp quad-cam 4.7-liter V-8. It drove the rear wheels through a five-speed ZF transaxle as used in Ford's GT40 endurance racers. In 1975, Maserati substituted its 4.9-liter 320-hp V-8 to compensate for power losses on emissions-regulated American models. This engine was standardized for Europe in 1976.

Suspension was independent coil all-round, steering was manual rack-and-pinion. Citroën had taken over Maserati in the mid-1960s and its presence showed in Bora's all-wheel disc-brake system, which was actuated by the French company's unique high-pressure hydraulics. The Bora used a conventional brake pedal rather than Citroën's mushroom-shaped button, but enjoyed the same "no-travel" action. All pedals were adjustable for reach—a first for any production car—and with the standard tilt/telescope steering wheel, air conditioning, and power windows, Bora was more accommodating than most Latin supercars.

Around town it could feel heavy and the engine, spitting and hacking at low revs, didn't seem to promise much, what with the modest 5500-rpm redline. But the Bora came alive in the hands of a smart, fast driver. Third gear was good for 118 mph and the communicative steering and well-sorted suspension made it, in *R&T*'s opinion, "one of the best-handling cars money can buy."

From 1972 through '83, Maserati sold a version of this car called the Merak with a V-6 engine that allowed for +2 rear seats. After Citroën sold out to Alejandro deTomaso in the mid-1970s, deTomaso kept both cars alive, but no improved versions were developed, leaving the Bora as the pinnacle of Maserati's roadgoing performance.

Maserati Bora
1971–1980

Wheelbase, in. 102.2

Weight, lbs. 3600

Price $25,500

Engine dohc V-8

Displacement liters/cu. in. 4.7/288

Fuel system 4 x 2 bbl. carburetors

Horsepower @ rpm 310 @ 6000

Torque @ rpm 325 @ 4200

Transmission 5-speed manual

Performance

0–60 mph, sec. 7.2

Top speed, mph 163

Maserati was quick to employ such advances as disc brakes and fuel injection, but was slow to move into mid-engine design. When finally it did, the Bora represented the marque with honor. Styling, by Giugiaro's Ital Design studio, was less radical than some rivals, but furnished more pleasing accommodations. The two-seat cockpit was well appointed and featured the world's first adjustable pedals, including a "no-travel" brake pedal. The glassy rear body section lifted to reveal a racing-derived quad-cam V-8. This 1973 model has the 4.7-liter version; later models used a 4.9. Low-speed performance was mediocre, but given its head, the Bora's well-sorted independent suspension and ample power delivered a thrilling ride. In total, just 571 Boras were produced.

MAZDA RX-7

*T*here are three significant things about the original RX-7. First, to the delight of enthusiasts everywhere, it revived the affordable sports car after the bloating of Datsun's 240Z. Second, it kept the rotary engine alive. Last and definitely not least, it was flat terrific.

Having made the rotary reliable—something Dr. Felix Wankel and his cohorts at NSU couldn't do—Mazda nearly went under during the first gas crisis by selling it in ordinary economy sedans. The rotary was more powerful than piston engines of similar displacement, but wasn't as fuel-efficient. Then Kenichi Yamamoto, the rotary's patron saint at Mazda, championed the rev-happy hummer as perfect for a reasonably priced sports car. Project X605 began in 1974, was completed by late '76, and went on sale in 1978 as the RX-7.

This was a conventional but thoroughly modern unibody hatchback coupe, with coil suspension and a live-rear-axle, recirculating-ball steering, and front-disc/rear-drum brakes. Styling mixed elements of several contemporary cars without looking like any one of them. The engine, of course, was what really made it special.

Breathing through a single four-barrel carb, Mazda's twin-rotor 12A Wankel spun 100 hp from just 1.1 liters. It was small enough to fit behind the front-wheel centerline and made for a finely balanced "front/mid-engine" design. Zero–60 mph came in 9.7 seconds, and top speed was 118. Zesty, nimble, and solidly built, the RX-7 was a sensational value at just $6995. It was a racer to be reckoned with, as well, dominating its IMSA classes and even challenging Corvettes and Porsches in theirs. *Road & Track* rightly declared it "an enthusiast's dream come true."

It wasn't perfect, certainly. The ride was a bit stiff, the cabin cramped for larger folks, and cornering got tail-happy on bumpy or wet surfaces. But the RX-7 was a hot seller from day one.

In 1981, the S and GS models were joined by the GSL; it had rear discs, a limited-slip diff, alloys, and power windows. Capping generation one was the GSL-SE, which bowed for 1984 and reeled 135 hp from its larger, fuel-injected 13B rotary while adding Pirelli P6s, larger brakes, and upgraded suspension.

Unfortunately, currency fluctuations had pushed RX-7 prices as high as $15,295 by then. The only consolation was that most rivals cost a lot more, and precious few could lay claim to being a minor classic.

After miscasting the rotary engine as an economy motor, Mazda found a home for it in a new sports car and gave birth to a minor classic. The original RX-7 blended elements of several contemporary rivals without looking like any one of them. Its compact twin-rotor Wankel was placed behind the front axle for optimal weight balance. Handling was sharp and horsepower—up to 135 in the fuel-injected version—came on smoothly. The RX-7 was a hit with critics and enthusiasts, and proved a successful race car. Relatively low pricing helped Mazda sell 505,000 examples of this first-generation model worldwide.

Mazda RX-7 GSL-SE
1984–1985

Wheelbase, in. 95.3

Weight, lbs. 2700

Price $15,100

Engine 2-rotor Wankel

Displacement liters/cu. in. 1.3/80

Fuel system Fuel injection

Horsepower @ rpm 135 @ 6000

Torque @ rpm 133 @ 2750

Transmission 5-speed manual

Performance

0–60 mph, sec. 8.5

Top speed, mph 128

MAZDA MX-5 MIATA

*F*orget the folderol about the Miata being an MG that doesn't leak oil. It stands on its own as a great sports car because it's simply a blast to drive.

The fuse was lit in the early 1980s, at Mazda's California design center, by auto-writer-turned-Mazda-product-planner Bob Hall and by stylist Mark Jordan, son of General Motors design director Chuck Jordan. Their idea for a classic front-engine rear-drive roadster beat Mazda-Japan's proposal for a "new-age" front-drive or mid-engine car. Work proceeded as a joint California-Tokyo project, and the resulting Miata exploded onto the market as a 1990 model.

Significantly, it was not parts-bin engineered, but was executed as an original design, a two-seat convertible laid down according to the sporting gospel of simplicity and lightweight. True, the basic 1.6-liter twincam engine could be traced to Mazda's 323 subcompact. But it was turned lengthwise, greatly reworked, and freed of its turbocharger. The rest of the car was fresh yet familiar, a timeless idea reinterpreted for our times.

Tidy in dimension and unsullied by geegaws, the body provided enough room for a couple of six footers and a night's soft luggage. The independent suspension used coil springs and double wishbones all-around. There was a disc brake at each corner and rack-and-pinion steering. The structure was impressively rigid thanks to computer-aided design and an aluminum powertrain truss. The top lowered in one easy motion, the ride was firm but not harsh, and the exhaust note appropriately snarly. You could order power steering and windows, a CD player and cruise control. But these weren't needed to enjoy the car. The Miata seemed to have achieved a rare blend of modest but fully usable power, accessible cornering limits, and all-around good cheer. Plus, it was leak-free, and Japanese-reliable, too.

An automatic transmission was available shortly after launch, and anti-lock brakes were options for '91. The engine grew to 1.8 liters and 128 hp for '94, and to 133 hp for '95. There was the club-racer R package and various luxury M editions, and base prices over the years went from under $14,000 to over $18,000. But nothing altered the Miata's character. It remains a communiqué from sports-car heaven.

Mazda MX-5 Miata
1990–

Wheelbase, in. 89.2

Weight, lbs. 2260

Price $13,800

Engine dohc I-4

Displacement liters/cu. in. 1.6/97

Fuel system Fuel injection

Horsepower @ rpm 116 @ 6500

Torque @ rpm 100 @ 5500

Transmission 5-speed manual

Performance

0–60 mph, sec. 9.2

Top speed, mph 116

Genuine landmarks are rare in the world of automobiles, but the Miata is one. Mazda showed enormous insight and sensitivity to the sports-car ethic when it designed a two-seater roadster free of unnecessary weight or features or even power. The appealing design is the result of a joint Japanese-American effort. It uses a purpose-made rear-drive chassis and a Mazda passenger-car four-cylinder reworked for this use. It went from an introductory 116 hp to 133 for '95, always just enough to keep performance lively. The simple cabin provides a great place to enjoy the fun.

MAZDA RX-7

*P*urity of purpose is as rare in a modern automobile as it is in modern life, which is why the third-generation RX-7 was a great sports car.

Mazda had followed the successful first-generation RX-7 with a plumper model dimmed by Porsche 924-derived styling. It was a more forgiving handler than the original and, with the addition of a 182-hp turbocharged rotary and convertible body, was faster and flashier. But it wasn't as sincere. Sports car or *boulevardier*? Mazda couldn't decide.

There was nothing ambiguous about the taut little two-place coupe that replaced it for 1993. Mazda went back to basics with a simpler, lighter, more potent, more entertaining RX-7. It had nothing in common with the 1986–1992 series except rear drive and the 1.3-liter Wankel. The Japanese automaker's California design team under Tom Matano had fashioned a genuine original, an organic form shrink-wrapped around tires, engine, and cockpit. Compared to its predecessor, the new RX-7 was 1.4 inches shorter, 1.4 inches lower, and 200 lbs lighter. Weight savings were everywhere—even the spark plug wires were the shortest possible length. The suspension was classic four-wheel double wishbone. The instruments clustered around the tachometer and, in time-honored sports-car tradition, were ringed in chrome.

The 13B rotary returned, but with two turbochargers acting in sequence; one provided boost at low- to medium-engine speeds, the other spooled up for high-rpm assaults. Lots of power and minimal mass is the foolproof formula for excitement, and the rotary rocket did not disappoint. Acceleration was swift, its moves were scalpel sharp. "It feels *connected* to the driver's senses," said *Road & Track*.

But there were flaws—a slight hesitation as the turbos transitioned; an interior of petite dimensions and ordinary materials; unreliable engine electronics; and an unduly stiff ride, particularly with the gymkhana-ready R1 option. Price was an obstacle, too—$31,300 to start—and insurance rates were prohibitive for many. Sales languished. Quality improved for '94, the suspension was softened, and a passenger-side air bag joined the driver-side restraint. But a strong yen pushed the base price to $34,000, and then to $37,500 for '95. Mazda was stuck with so many unsold '95s it simply didn't import the car for 1996. In every market but Japan, the RX-7 was dead, a martyr to pure performance in an imperfect world.

Mazda RX-7
1993–1995

Wheelbase, in. 95.5

Weight, lbs. 2800

Price $31,300

Engine Twin turbo 2-rotor Wankel

Displacement liters/cu. in. 1.3/80

Fuel system Fuel injection

Horsepower @ rpm 255 @ 6500

Torque @ rpm 217 @ 5000

Transmission 5-speed manual

Performance

0–60 mph, sec. 5.3

Top speed, mph 157

Mazda's third-generation RX-7 restored the rotary rocket as a premier sports car. Most anything detracting from performance was discarded. The body stretched tight over the tires and cockpit. Ovoid portals led to a cabin of cozy dimensions, but drilled pedals and bright gauge bezels signaled the car's purpose. Handling was sharp, but the ride unforgiving. Weight was pared and the twin-turbo Wankle packed 255 hp. All this purposefulness went for naught when high prices and other factors killed the RX-7.

McLaren F1

*M*otoring journals aren't as shy as they ought to be about declaring their latest cover subject the greatest supercar of all time. If such a distinction is possible, however, it likely rests with the McLaren F1.

In capability (231-mph top speed), imaginative design (a central driving position), and extravagant price ($810,000), the F1 stands alone. Revealed to the public in May 1992, it was on the road by 1994, and in the winner's circle at LeMans in 1995. "[I]ts performance and general ability simply defy imagination," wrote journalist Paul Frere, a former Formula 1 driver and LeMans winner.

Drawing on multiple Formula 1, CanAm, and Indianapolis victories, the McLaren organization set about creating its first road car in 1989. The F1 was a clean-sheet design, with all components except the taillamps built specifically for it. The guiding principle was efficiency. Thus it is compact, with body panels and understructure of featherweight carbon fiber, and virtually every mechanical component of aluminum or magnesium.

BMW Motorsports was contracted to design and build the engine, which McLaren specified be naturally aspirated for instant response. With its mid-ships 48-valve 6.1-liter V-12 and under four pounds per horsepower, the F1 has the best power-to-weight ratio ever in a production road car. Manual steering and brakes further enhance control. Small electric underbody fans generate ground-effects grip that renders four-wheel drive superfluous, and a modest rear spoiler deploys to counteract nosedive in hard braking.

The driver's seat is personally fitted to each owner and is placed centrally for optimal command without intrusion from wheel arches or the nuisance of offset pedals. A passenger seat is mounted to each side and slightly behind. Air conditioning, CD audio system, and the finest leathers complete the cabin.

Incredibly, some specifications had to be *scaled back* for LeMans. Even with nonactive aerodynamics and engine-intake restrictions, the 220-mph GTR competition version took first, third, fourth, and fifth overall against a slew of purpose-built racers.

"[T]he McLaren offers engineering and workmanship second to none and performance never attained before in a road car," concluded Frere in his 1994 *Road & Track* cover story entitled, without apology, "The Best Ever!"

Built to exceed every previous sports car in performance and driver control, the McClaren F1 is a no-compromise, $1-million road car that raced—and won—at LeMans. Carbon-fiber body and chassis construction and aluminum and magnesium mechanicals team with a BMW V-12 engine for an unprecedented power-to-weight ratio. Scissor-type doors provide access to a leather-lined interior with a "1+2" layout: The driver is centrally located in a formfitting seat, with room for passengers on either side.

McClaren F1
1994–

Wheelbase, in. 107.0

Weight, lbs. 2244

Price $810,000

Engine dohc V-12

Displacement liters/cu. in. 6.1/370

Fuel system Fuel injection

Horsepower @ rpm 627 @ 7000

Torque @ rpm 500 @ 5600

Transmission 6-speed manual

Performance

0–60 mph, sec. 3.2

Top speed, mph 231

MERCEDES-BENZ 300SL

*O*ver time, impressions of the classic Ferraris, Jaguars, Lamborghinis, and Porsches tend to swirl into a single golden sports-car memory, their pecking order indistinct. But step back into the mid-1950s, and it's clear the Mercedes-Benz 300SL was in an orbit of its own.

"We can state unequivocally . . . the 300SL coupe is the ultimate in an all-round sports car," said *Road & Track* in April 1955. Gushed Walt Woron in the July 1956 *Motor Trend*, "If there's a better production sports car in the world than the 300SL, show me the way to it!" Only Ferrari approached such accolades, but it couldn't blend around-town gentility with open-road speed the way the 300SL could, and it certainly couldn't match the Benz's impeccable workmanship or even its unique design.

S for Super, L for Light, 300 for the engine's 3.0 liters, the 300SL was conceived not as a road car but as a 1952 sports-racer. It promptly took first and second in the Carrera Panamericana, the 24 Hours of LeMans, and the Nürburgring 1000 Kilometers. American import baron Max Hoffman convinced Mercedes to issue a production version, which it did in 1954.

The steel and aluminum bodies employed a robust frame of triangulated tubes. The structure's tall sills precluded ordinary doors, necessitating the top-hinged "gullwing" portals that were the coupe's signature design feature.

The inline-six was drawn from that of the big Mercedes 300 sedan, but was canted 50 degrees left to clear the SL's hood. It was made of aluminum, used Bosch mechanical fuel injection, and had 220 hp—54 *more* than the LeMans-winning version. An optional cam brought 240. This flexible six worked through an all-synchro four-speed and propelled the most-aerodynamic road car of its day to 140 mph with the 3.42:1 gearing, and to near 160 with the available 3.25:1. A coil suspension furnished a stable ride and spirited handling, but swing rear axles could prompt vicious oversteer.

In 1957, Mercedes replaced the Gullwing with the 300SL Roadster. Its modified space frame permitted conventional doors and its reworked rear suspension was friendlier at the limit; it was built through 1963. Time has softened the impact of the Gullwing, but to the sports-car enthusiast of the mid-1950s, nothing else could touch it.

The great 300SL was a LeMans-winner brought to the road. The high sills of its tube frame necessitated top-hinged doors for the celebrated "gullwing" effect. Its fuel-injected inline-six took 16 quarts of oil and produced a peerless blend of power and poise. Fitted luggage was appropriately toney. Mercedes built 1400 coupe and 1858 convertible 300SLs.

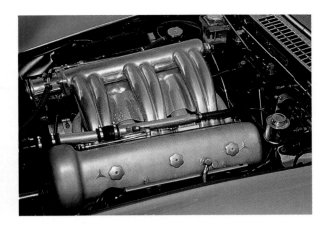

Mercedes-Benz 300SL
1954–1957

Wheelbase, in. 94.5

Weight, lbs. 2710

Price $7500

Engine sohc I-6

Displacement liters/cu. in. 3.0/183

Fuel system Fuel injection

Horsepower @ rpm 240 @ 5800

Torque @ rpm 202 @ 4000

Transmission 4-speed manual

Performance

0–60 mph, sec. 7.4

Top speed, mph 140

MERCEDES-BENZ 190SL

*T*he 1950s sports-car establishment never could come to terms with this aristocratic European.

It had the proper sporting cues: dashing two-seat styling; all-independent coil-sprung suspension; floorshifted four-speed; even a slightly temperamental overhead-cam four-cylinder engine. But cars of this specification—and this price—were supposed to rip out to the road course on the weekend, go fender-to-fender with XK 120s, then terrorize the populace on the way home. Ferraris could. Porsches could. But this roadster from mighty Mercedes-Benz could not.

"It's a dull-but-expensive piece of transportation in sports car clothing," wrote Jerry Titus in *Sports Car Graphic*. "While this opinion may infuriate some proud 190 owners, we doubt it will even raise an eyebrow at the factory, as we suspect this is exactly what they had in mind."

Precisely. Daimler-Benz had made a remarkable postwar recovery, rising from Stuttgart's bombed rubble to resume auto and truck production and even to go racing in 1952 with the purpose-built 300SL. Road versions of that competition coupe reached showrooms about the same time as the

190SL, which was styled inside and out to resemble the exotic 300, but was never intended to duplicate its performance.

Like most sports cars of the day, the 190SL was bred from a sedan platform. Its engine was tweaked with twin Solex carbs, but they were difficult to adjust and power was only adequate for the car's weight. The suspension, tuned to fight the snap-oversteer tendency of M-B's swing rear axles, delivered a compliant ride and relatively modest cornering. There was a removable steel hardtop option, and eventually, a fixed-roof coupe. In all of them, passenger and luggage space were unusually generous for a two-seater, and workmanship was of the highest order.

Judged as the sports tourer it was designed to be, the 190SL delivered at least as much as it promised. In fact, said *Motorsport* in 1956, "Proper use of the gears will propel a 190SL faster than most pilots can safely drive, and they will survive thanks to an overall dynamically balanced design." By 1963, Mercedes would offer only one two-seater, the "pagoda-roof" 230SL. It was more like the suave 190 than the fierce 300, settling any debate about the sports-car philosophy of this German giant.

Mercedes-Benz 190SL
1955–1963

Wheelbase, in. 94.5

Weight, lbs. 2558

Price $5,800

Engine sohc I-4

Displacement liters/cu. in. 1.9/116

Fuel system 2 x 2 bbl. carburetors

Horsepower @ rpm 120 @ 5800

Torque @ rpm 137 @ 3500

Transmission 4-speed manual

Performance

0–60 mph, sec. 12.0

Top speed, mph 101

The 190SL resembled the 300SL, but didn't have gullwing doors or supercar performance. It was a "gentleman's" sports car that was nonetheless more than a match for most gentlemen drivers.

MERCEDES-BENZ SLK

*T*wo-seat roadsters from Mercedes-Benz grew less sports-car-like after the original 190 and 300. By the late 1990s, the flagship SL600 was a $120,100, 4455-lb luxo-cruiser with a 389-hp 6.0-liter V-12. It could do 0–60 mph in 5.9 seconds and run at 155 mph, but even Mercedes didn't call it a sports car. It called the new SLK a sports car.

Translated from German, SLK is an acronym meaning "Sporty, Light, and Short." Introduced to America in early 1997, this roadster is Mercedes's answer to the BMW Z3 and Porsche Boxster, and is distinguished from both by its engine and roof.

The SLK rides a shortened Mercedes C-class sedan platform and has a new, all-steel body. Retaining the compact sedan's independent suspension and generous wheel travel gives it good ride quality, while judiciously firming up the damping, replacing recirculating-ball steering with rack-and-pinion, and fitting more aggressive tires—wider in back than in front—produces curve-hugging handling.

The most unique feature is a fully automatic retracting hardtop. Pushing one button transforms the SLK from a closed coupe to an open convertible in 25 seconds. The electrohydraulic roof cleaves at the rear pillars, the trunklid opens backward, and the top retracts into a rear compartment. The trunklid then works conventionally, though luggage space shrinks from 12.3 cubic feet to 5.1 with the roof stowed. Still, the roof gives the SLK weather protection, security, and a conversation piece its rivals don't have.

"Kompressor" fender script signals presence of a "compressor," making this the first supercharged Mercedes since the 1930s. The crankshaft-driven blower fortifies a 2.3-liter iron-block, aluminum-head four-cylinder. European SLKs can have a naturally aspirated 136-hp 2.0 four-cylinder and a five-speed manual gearbox, but all U.S. cars get the supercharged 2.3 and a five-speed automatic that electronically adjusts shifts to suit driving style. The American combination produces fine power through a wide rpm range. There's little supercharger whine, but the exhaust emits a swaggering snarl. Simulated carbon-fiber interior trim substitutes for traditional Mercedes wood. Tube bars behind each seat offer rollover protection, and a special child seat is available that disarms the passenger-side air bag. Forty-three years after the original SLs helped rejuvenate one of the world's great automakers, Mercedes-Benz is back in the sports-car business.

Mercedes returned to sports cars on its own terms with the SLK. All U.S. models use a supercharged 2.3-liter twincam four and and automatic transmission. The hardtop folds and stows automatically to change the two-seater from coupe to convertible.

Mercedes-Benz SLK230
1997–

Wheelbase, in. 94.5

Weight, lbs. 2922

Price $40,000

Engine Supercharged dohc I-4

Displacement liters/cu. in. 2.3/140

Fuel system Fuel injection

Horsepower @ rpm 191 @ 5300

Torque @ rpm 206 @ 2500

Transmission 5-speed automatic

Performance

0–60 mph, sec. 7.2

Top speed, mph 142

MG TC

The MG TC seemed hardly the sort of thing to spark a revolution. It was already quite outmoded when announced in 1945 as one of Britain's first postwar cars. It was only mildly evolved from MG's prewar TA/TB roadsters, which themselves weren't very different from the first Morris Garages car of 1923. But the TC, as later MG ads proclaimed, was "the sports car America loved first," and things haven't been the same since.

World War II GIs were the first Americans to discover the charms of sporting European cars, MGs included. And the TC was available factory fresh at war's end, so a good many Yanks took one home, where they spread the gospel that getting there could be more than half the fun. Soon, sports cars began capturing America's fancy—if not many sales—with the TC a symbol of the budding enthusiasm.

Still, these were very "foreign" cars to a people weaned on big engines, futuristic styling, and gee-whiz technology, and the TC was a frank anachronism with its flexible ladder-type chassis, crude solid-axle suspension, floorshift gearbox and tiny (but tough) four-cylinder engine. Yet like Ford's Model

T, Americans loved this MG in spite of its faults, maybe even *because* of them. As *Road & Track* founder John Bond wrote in 1956: "For a comfort-loving public [it] was wretchedly impractical; your spine was jolted, your knees bumped, you were hot in the sun and wet in the rain, you had no luggage space and only 54 hp—but for the first time in many a year you were driving a car. A person felt it was part of him, as quick and responsive to commands as a well trained mare, and for many a U.S. driver this was something new and wonderful." And, of course, it looked terrific: classically "correct," rakish yet elegant—English decorum with wire wheels and cutaway doors.

In retrospect, the TC was fortuitously timed for a postwar America with money to burn and time to spare. Who cared that performance was leisurely or that the skimpy top defied all operating logic? This was a car for sunny days and roads less traveled, one you drove for the sheer pleasure of it, not just to go somewhere. Old-fashioned it may have been, but the MG TC helped make driving a new American sport, and in the late 1940s, that was revolution indeed.

MG TC
1945–1949

Wheelbase, in. 94.0

Weight, lbs. 1735

Price $2150

Engine ohv I-4

Displacement liters/cu. in. 1.25/76.3

Fuel system 2 x 1 bbl. carburetors

Horsepower @ rpm 54 @ 5200

Torque @ rpm 63 @ 3000

Transmission 4-speed manual

Performance

0–60 mph, sec. 22.7

Top speed, mph 75

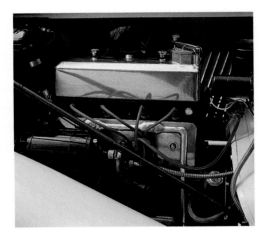

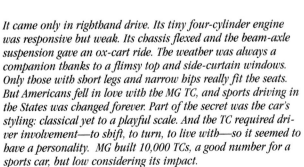

It came only in righthand drive. Its tiny four-cylinder engine was responsive but weak. Its chassis flexed and the beam-axle suspension gave an ox-cart ride. The weather was always a companion thanks to a flimsy top and side-curtain windows. Only those with short legs and narrow hips really fit the seats. But Americans fell in love with the MG TC, and sports driving in the States was changed forever. Part of the secret was the car's styling: classical yet to a playful scale. And the TC required driver involvement—to shift, to turn, to live with—so it seemed to have a personality. MG built 10,000 TCs, a good number for a sports car, but low considering its impact.

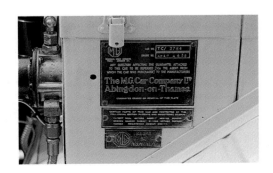

MG TD

Purists once bemoaned the MG TD as the beginning of the end for the classic British sports car. In fact, the TD was the inevitable first step toward a more modern postwar MG capable of earning serious money abroad, which in 1949 meant mainly the lucrative U.S. market. As marque expert Richard Knudson observed: "If the TC started the sports car revolution, it was the TD that fought the battle."

It did so by improving on the TC without losing its charm. Styling, for instance, continued Edwardian themes: bolt-upright radiator, cutaway doors, flowing separate fenders, fold-flat windscreen, a diabolical top and side curtains providing casual weather protection at best. Even so, exterior metal was all new, and although the inner body still relied on 1920s-style wood framing, the TD was a bit wider and thus roomier than the TC, if still quite cramped. It was also some 200 lbs heavier, and as power was unchanged, acceleration was down though top speed was up.

Two changes were instantly apparent: The TC had righthand drive only while the TD was lefthand drive from day one; and the TD had 15-inch steel wheels instead of stately 19-inch wires, a cost-cut that some enthusiasts deemed sacrilege.

Happily, those wheels attached to a stronger frame with the relatively startling advance of independent front suspension. This came from MG's new 1949 Y-Series sedan, though with wheelbase trimmed to TC length. Another chassis "innovation" was a kickup in the rear siderails allowing more wheel travel. That combined with softer damping, wider tires, the reduced height from the smaller wheels, and the new coil-sprung front to furnish a smoother ride and even tauter handling. If an evident concession to American tastes, the TD proved the most popular sporting MG yet, outpacing TC production by nearly 3–1 over the same four-year lifespan. Tellingly, more than two-thirds (precisely 23,488) were sold in the United States.

The TD was a favored "club racer" like the TC, so the "TD II" was a welcome mid-1951 development, boasting a larger clutch and oil pan, plus other minor but useful updates. MG also encouraged TD racers by offering various suspension and engine kits, as well as a short-lived 60-hp special, the "TD Mark II." By late 1953, however, Triumph's truly modern TR2 had MG looking to its laurels on the track and in the showroom. As a result, the TD stepped aside for an even more "radical" MG that would have those diehards grousing anew.

MG TD
1949–1953

Wheelbase, in. 94.0

Weight, lbs. 1930

Price $2200

Engine ohv I-4

Displacement liters/cu. in. 1.25/76.3

Fuel system 2 x 1 bbl. carburetors

Horsepower @ rpm 54 @ 5200

Torque @ rpm 63 @ 3000

Transmission 4-speed manual

Performance

0–60 mph, sec. 24.1

Top speed, mph 80

The MG TC opened America's doors to the affordable British sports car, and the TD stepped in. Production of this TC successor reached 29,664, and about 90 percent of them had lefthand drive. MG wisely didn't overhaul the styling, though 19-inch wire wheels did go in favor of less-charming but better-handling 15-inch steel discs. Road manners further improved thanks to the move to independent front suspension and a strengthened frame. The TD was roomier but heavier than the TC, and with no more power, not as spry, though top speed was a bit higher.

MG TF-1500

What does an MG TF-1500 have in common with a '57 Chevy? Not much, you may say. One was a small, stark, British Traditional roadster, the other a big, flashy period Detroiter with creature comforts galore and a plethora of body styles.

But consider: Both were basically extensions of existing cars given more power and updated styling to fend off all-new rivals. More significantly, each was the last and arguably the best of a kind. No surprise, then, that both have become the most coveted of their breeds, in part because each ended an era and not everyone liked what followed.

The TF succeeded the TD (MG skipped "TE" for sounding like "tee hee") and was essentially a streamlined version of it. With fared headlamps, downsloped hood, raked grille, and lean-forward tail, it looked like what MG might have sold had not World War II intervened. But the TF didn't appear until late 1953, by which time the T-Series was way outclassed by new-design sports cars of similar price—mainly the thoroughly modern Triumph TR2. Though MG coaxed 3 hp more, or

57 total, from its veteran 1250cc engine, the TF was no match for the 90-hp TR and was little faster than a TD, despite its smoother styling.

Then again, it was only a stopgap. MG had actually designed the T-Series' eventual successor by 1952, when it became part of the big new British Motor Corporation. But BMC was soon occupied with another new sports car, the Austin-Healey, so the future MGA was temporarily shelved and the TF was left to meet critical press reviews and slow sales (6200 built). MG responded by installing a 1466cc engine with 10 percent more power and 17 percent more torque to create the TF-1500 of 1954. Though quicker than the 1250 TF by 2.5 seconds to 60 mph and 5 mph all out, the 85-mph 1500 still was no threat to the 105-mph Triumph.

No matter. This turned out to be a one-year holding action of no great consequence—at the time. It's a different story now, as TF-1500s command top price among postwar Ts, equal to and sometimes above those of the classic TC. Which only proves that the last can be first in enthusiast affections, particularly when it's scarce to begin with.

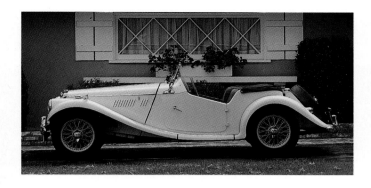

MG needed a new sports car to fight the likes of the Austin-Healey and Triumph TR2, but its owners forced it to update the aged TD. The resulting TF had an old-world flavor that didn't sell and old-school mechanicals that didn't perform. MG built 6200 TFs with the 1259cc engine and another 3400 as 1.5-liter "1500" models, the latter now the most sought-after of the MG T series. The TF-1500 pictured has an aftermarket steering wheel.

MG TF-1500
1954–1955

Wheelbase, in. 94.0

Weight, lbs. 1930

Price $2000

Engine ohv I-4

Displacement liters/cu. in. 1.5/89.5

Fuel system 2 x 1 bbl. carburetors

Horsepower @ rpm 63 @ 5000

Torque @ rpm 76 @ 3000

Transmission 4-speed manual

Performance

0–60 mph, sec. 16.3

Top speed, mph 85

MGA TWIN CAM

After so many years of old-fashioned MGs, the MGA of 1955 was like something from another world. And in one sense it was: an early product of British Motor Corporation's brave new world of cost-conscious parts-bin engineering. Nevertheless, the A was an exciting, thoroughly competitive postwar MG sports car. Today it's an honored classic.

The MGA served to introduce several components destined for many future BMC cars, notably a rugged new "B-Series" overhead-valve four-cylinder engine and associated four-speed gearbox. Features unique to the sports car included a massively strong new chassis, albeit with TD/TF-type independent front suspension. And—finally—there was an all-steel body with curvy, well-proportioned lines as modern as anything on the road. Though tradition was served by the usual two-seat roadster, again with side curtains and an improved but still difficult top, a companion "bubbletop" coupe soon arrived with curved glass fore and aft, plus—blimey!—rollup door windows.

Early MGAs were 72-hp "1500s," but 1959 introduced a 1.6-liter engine with 80 hp. Two years later, the 1600 became a Mark II with adoption of front disc brakes (drums continued aft) and more upright vertical

grille bars. A stronger engine had always been planned, and it belatedly arrived in mid-1958 for special "1600 Twin Cam" models with standard all-disc brakes and center-lock alloy wheels. Though cylinder size was unchanged from the ohv unit, the Twin Cam had its own alloy head with hemispherical combustion chambers and a high-for-the-day 9.9:1 compression ratio. These and assorted other tweaks added 28 hp, boosting top speed to at least 110 mph.

Unfortunately, the Twin Cam suffered serious knocking on ordinary fuel and, though a fierce performer when running right, it fast became known as a heavy oil-user. Add in a hefty $850 surcharge over comparable ohv models, and it's little wonder that sales started poorly and got worse.

MG gave up in early 1960 at only 2111 examples, ironically just after curing the oil-burning and detonation problems. Leftover chassis were given pushrod engines and sold as "Deluxe" models. Of these, only 82 were "Mark I" roadsters and coupes; another 313 were Mark IIs. Overall, though, the MGA series was a resounding success, with some 101,000 built in seven years, more than double the number of T-Series MGs produced over two decades.

MGA Twin Cam
1958–1960

Wheelbase, in. 94.0

Weight, lbs. 2200

Price $3345

Engine dohc I-4

Displacement liters/cu. in. 1.6/97

Fuel system 2 x 1 bbl. carburetors

Horsepower @ rpm 108 @ 6700

Torque @ rpm 104 @ 4500

Transmission 4-speed manual

Performance

0–60 mph, sec. 9.9

Top speed, mph 113

MG burst into modern sports car design with the MGA of 1955. Its envelope body was smartly styled and featured roll-up windows. Performance was credible and the fun was back. The Twin Cam version arrived in '58 as the first dohc production MG. It had better power and four disc brakes, but was plagued by poor engine reliability.

MGB

*T*he MGB was remarkably long-lived, continuing without basic change through 18 years and over half a million units. Of course, its maker could hardly have imagined such longevity when launching the B in 1962 to replace the popular MGA, itself the first sports car to break 100,000 production. Yet even then, there was something in the B's simple lines, stout mechanical heart, and rugged-yet-cheery character to suggest this MG would be a car for the ages.

The B was certainly that, even though post-1974 models were increasingly compromised in style, performance, and desirability by patchwork solutions to U.S. safety and emissions rules. Not that there's anything wrong with a B GT, the neat hatchback coupe version announced in 1965 and sold through the bitter end in 1980. But without question, the 1960s roadsters were the purest and most satisfying of the breed.

Technically, the open B was a convertible, as it had wind-down windows (to the chagrin of many MG fans) and, eventually, a folding top fixed to the body. But as an MG, the B was definitely a sports car. It was also a better MG,

with the marque's first unitized body, and more cockpit space than the MGA despite a three-inch shorter wheelbase. Under the bonnet buzzed an upsized 1.8-liter "B-Series" four, which became smoother and stronger in late 1964 with a switch from three to five main bearings. Horsepower through 1974 was 95, delivered to a four-speed gearbox with available electric overdrive, making this the first MG capable of keeping pace with rival Triumphs. Steering, brakes, and suspension were also from the A and thus rather dated, but they made for foolproof handling and a surprisingly supple sports-car ride.

In 1967, the B was treated to a "Mark II" update featuring a new grille, synchronized first gear—at last—and MG's first automatic transmission, a rare option with only about 5000 fitted. It then soldiered on with little change until its depressing "federalization" of 1975–80, which created cars even MG fans didn't warm to. But early Bs still engender great affection, one reason lovingly cared-for examples remain a common sight today. That's the way it is with MGs, and probably always will be.

MGB
1962–1971

Wheelbase, in. 91.0

Weight, lbs. 2030

Price $2800

Engine ohv I-4

Displacement liters/cu. in. 1.8/110

Fuel system 2 x 1 bbl. carburetors

Horsepower @ rpm 95 @ 5500

Torque @ rpm 107 @ 3500

Transmission 4-speed manual

Performance

0–60 mph, sec. 13.0

Top speed, mph 95

A bigger hit than the MGA was the MGB. Styling, by MG's staff, was cleaner and looks right even today. This was MG's first unit-body construction, but the B really was mechanically ordinary. Still, the torquey ohv four packed satisfying punch. And the suspension, derived from the MGA and fortified by standard front disc brakes, provided fine handling. This was how a '60s sports car ought to look and feel, though it was a dated performer by the '70s. MG sold more than 500,000 MGBs, including B GT coupes styled with help from Pininfarina. Tools were provided for the genuine knock-off wheels, but the wood dash trim on this car is not original equipment.

MG RV8

*T*he "R" in RV8 stands for Rover, and thereby hangs this tale. In 1968, when the MGB was but six years old, its maker, British Motor Corporation, combined with Leyland Motors, home of Triumph and Rover, to form British Leyland. BL could do little right. By the mid-1980s, a string of unhappy cars and crippling sales losses had reduced a once-broad stable of makes to just Austin and Rover. By 1990, only Rover was left.

The beloved MGB was then a decade dead, but demand for replacement parts remained strong. One day, two British enthusiasts stumbled upon 1000 tons of original B tooling, including jigs and dies for making complete bodies. Rover was only too happy to sell, so the pair bought the lot and founded British Motor Heritage to serve dedicated B-keepers under Rover auspices. Meanwhile, the success of Mazda's Miata had Rover pondering a return to sports cars. With retro roadsters hot and BMH established, a revived MGB was a natural.

Enter the RV8, in 1993, as an updated open version of the 1973–76 B GT V8, a low-volume Britain-only coupe model. Although the V-8 here was a 3.9-liter from the posh Range Rover, it stemmed from the same all-aluminum ohv Buick design that Rover acquired in the late '60s. Restyled body panels (save doors and trunklid) freshened the traditional B appearance, but the RV8 chassis was pure 1962 except for telescopic shocks replacing antique lever-arm dampers. Wheels, tires, and dash also were modernized, and the cockpit was swathed in leather and walnut worthy of a Jaguar. Unfortunately, expected 1990s features such as power assists and anti-lock brakes were conspicuously absent considering the stiff $40,000 price. Predictably, familiar old B failings were now present in the fastest production MG ever. *Autocar* magazine was typical of the British press in calling the RV8 "an anachronism, albeit a strangely likeable one . . . easy to enjoy and even fun to drive in an agricultural, vintage manner." But good value? Hardly.

Still, Rover had no trouble selling the modest 2000 RV8s it planned to build; interestingly, about half went to Japan. All had righthand drive, and this, plus the lack of several required safety items, precluded U.S. sales. The MG sports car had risen from the grave, and there was more to come.

MG RV8
1993–1994

Wheelbase, in. 92.0

Weight, lbs. 2430

Price $40,000

Engine ohv V-8

Displacement liters/cu. in. 3.9/241

Fuel system Fuel injection

Horsepower @ rpm 190 @ 4750

Torque @ rpm 234 @ 3200

Transmission 5-speed manual

Performance

0–60 mph, sec. 6.9

Top speed, mph 136

Rover teamed with a British privateer to create a new-but-familiar-looking MG. The RV8 put fresh and vintage MGB bodywork over a '60s-era MG chassis. The cabin got more leather and wood than any MG ever had, and a Rover V-8 (from a '60s Buick design) made it the fastest production MG ever.

MGF

*M*any cars claim to be "all-new," but the MGF truly is. Aside from two seats, folding top, and the hallowed octagon badge, it owes nothing to past MGs. It's a sports car of and for the '90s—and one of the best around. Given MG's sad state in the '80s, the F is both a welcome rebirth and an unexpected revolution.

It originated five years after the final B, when MG limped along with just a few sporty sedans based on humdrum Austins. But Austin Rover hadn't abandoned "real" MGs, and hinted as much with the 1985 EX-E concept, a stylish mid-engine coupe. Four years later, a new sporting MG dubbed "Phoenix Revival" was underway at the successor Rover Group. Though this program considered front- and rear-drive layouts, mid-engine/rear drive was finally chosen for reasons of handling and image, with Toyota's then-new MR2 the benchmark for performance, packaging, and refinement. Design work was mostly finished by 1992, when Rover was bought by prosperous BMW, thus assuring the new model's future.

The result was a smooth compact convertible with an exceptionally rigid unit-steel structure and MG's first all-independent suspension. The latter was effective but not entirely new, being evolved from the novel "Hydragas" spring/damper system pioneered by the hapless mid-'70s Austin Allegro sedan. Sideways behind the cockpit sat an upsized version of Rover's new K-series passenger-car engine, an advanced all-alloy four with twincams and 16 valves. Unique to the F was sophisticated variable valve timing that improved horsepower from 120 on the base model to 145 for the uplevel VVC edition, which also boasted a nifty new electric power steering system (optional on the base model).

With performance, comfort, and quality virtually unknown to MGs, the F met with instant wide acclaim. Predictably perhaps, Britain's *Car* magazine picked the VVC over the new BMW Z3 and front-drive Alfa Spider in a May 1996 showdown: "The MG gleefully attacks bends, tires biting, engine sizzling . . . [It] not only does the job better than its rivals here, it has actually redefined the job. It does brilliantly what a sports car should do."

Alas, the F won't do anything in America, locked out by U.S. safety and emissions rules. Happily, Rover is already working on the next sporting MG, which *will* come Stateside and could be even better than the F.

MGF VVC
1995–

Wheelbase, in. 93.7

Weight, lbs. 2360

Price $28,500

Engine dohc I-4

Displacement liters/cu. in. 1.8/110

Fuel system Fuel injection

Horsepower @ rpm 145 @ 7000

Torque @ rpm 128 @ 4500

Transmission 5-speed manual

Performance

0–60 mph, sec. 7.0

Top speed, mph 130

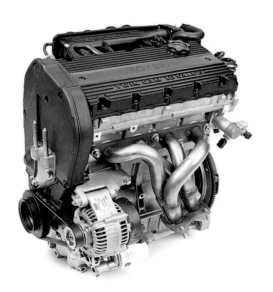

The MG for the 1990s and beyond has the same two-seat roadster spirit as its best predecessors, but alters the formula to include the marque's first midships engine and all-independent suspension. The MGF's styling is chunky, but packages comfortable seating for two and generous cargo room. Mounted transversely behind the cockpit is a Rover-built all-alloy 1.8-liter twincam four with variable valve timing and up to 145 hp.

MORGAN PLUS 4

*L*ike Henry Ford, Henry Frederick Stanley Morgan dreamed of making his fortune with a cheap universal car—only he lived in England, where "proper" automobiles were heavily taxed. He thus turned to tax-free cyclecars: small, three-wheel roadsters with two-cylinder motorcycle engines and brisk performance. What set the Morgan apart from other cyclecars was its independent front suspension by a simple sliding-pillar design, a genuine revolution for solid-axle 1910.

Morgan prospered through the '20s as one of Britain's most affordable cars before being eclipsed by cheap four-wheelers from giants Austin and Morris. But the rugged tricycle "Moggies" remained a force in competition, and their sales appeal shifted from basic transport to winning sports car, a reputation that persisted through the last of the line in 1952.

By that point, Morgan's mainstay was a "proper" sports car called the 4/4 (4 wheels/4 cylinders), new in 1935 but remarkably little changed since. By the '50s it was as antique as an MG-TC, with an ash-framed body and hard sliding-pillar suspension, yet HFS and his son Peter refused to change it. Happily, the 4/4 charmed enough Americans

that tiny Morgan prospered anew with its old-fashioned cars.

But even Morgan wasn't entirely immune to change, and in 1951 it issued the Plus 4. Aimed mainly at wealthy Americans, this was a deluxe replacement for the 4/4 (which would return in 1956). It had a longer wheelbase, belated hydraulic brakes, and instead of a mild 1.3-liter four, a 2.1-liter Standard engine from that firm's new 1948 Vanguard sedan. A four-seat roadster soon joined the traditional two-seater, as did two- and four-place "drophead" convertibles. Styling then evolved a bit in 1954, as the flat-faced radiator gave way to a domed vertical-bar grille. Also that year came a more potent engine option, the 95-hp version developed for Standard-Triumph's own sporting TRs. This was the Plus 4's only engine by 1959, when wider bodies with faired-in headlamps appeared, along with optional front disc brakes. The last were standard by 1962, as was a modernized engine with 105 hp or, in rare Super Sports tune, 115–120 hp.

The Plus 4 vanished after 1969, then returned in the late '80s for Britain and Europe with a new engine and updated interior. But that's Morgan for you: changing yet changeless—not unlike jolly old England herself.

This is a 1961 Morgan Plus 4, but it's hardly distinguishable from a '54 model or a '69. For that matter, its basic chassis and ash-framed body can be traced directly to the original four-wheel Morgan of the 1930s. That of course is the magic of Morgan, the new-old British sports car with the cult following. This small, family-owned manufacturer builds fewer cars than it can sell, thereby fueling demand. The TR pictured is an example of the model that helped endear the Plus 4 to enthusiasts by employing a succession of Triumph engines. Outright speed was not the issue, a vintage sports-car feel was, and with its cut-down doors and spartan cockpit, the Plus 4 delivered.

MORGAN PLUS 8

*L*ike every Morgan, the Plus 8 offers elemental motoring at its best—and worst. That means a cramped, leaky, stiff-riding sports car, but one with super-responsive handling and an old-time driving feel no modern car can duplicate. It also means resolutely 1930s styling—Morgans were "retro" decades ago—plus patient handwork by virtuoso artists in wood, metal, and leather. Like every Morgan since the '20s, the Plus 8 issues from the quaint Pickersleigh Road shops set up by HFS Morgan himself in the Worchestershire hamlet of Malvern Link. And though neither the company nor its cars have essentially changed over the years, Morgans have become quite costly, in part because demand far exceeds supply. Want a new one? Order now, then wait five years.

What's special about the Plus 8 is that it delivers everything Morgan at much higher velocities. That's because it has a V-8, the same all-aluminum pushrod design that was born at Buick and adopted by Rover. Actually, the 8 was a child of necessity, evolved from the Plus 4 to replace that model when its Triumph-sourced engine was discontinued.

Luckily, the V-8 was an easy fit, requiring just a two-inch-longer wheelbase and a slightly wider chassis. Better still, it was little heavier than the old four yet packed nearly 50 percent more power. Add in modest overall weight and you have a "veddy British" roadster that can out-drag some Ferraris. Top speed? It's now an alleged 130 mph despite the vintage "aerodynamics," but only fools would attempt that. Morgans have always been best in top-down touring on smooth, snaky roads at up to, say, 80 mph; this one merely gets there a lot quicker.

Today's Plus 8 is basically the debut 1968 model, but axles and fenders have been widened a couple times, and performance improved by a mid-'80s switch from carburetors to fuel injection, then more displacement (from 3.5 liters to 3.9). Though U.S. imports have been spotty since 1972 (blame safety and emissions laws), street-legal 8s are again available to determined Yanks with deep pockets.

Twenty years ago, *Road & Track* described the Plus 8 as being all about "romance—young love, moonlit motoring on winding blacktop roads and coffee stops in unlikely places. A car for F. Scott Fitzgerald heroes and heroines, yet surely as appealing to the pot generation. . ." That's still true, thank goodness. We'd all be poorer without this defiantly individual new-old car.

Morgan Plus 8 "3.9" 1968–

Wheelbase, in. 98.0

Weight, lbs. 1900

Price $46,000

Engine ohv V-8

Displacement liters/cu. in. 3.9/241

Fuel system Fuel injection

Horsepower @ rpm 190 @ 4750

Torque @ rpm 230 @ 2600

Transmission 5-speed manual

Performance

0–60 mph, sec. 5.6

Top speed, mph 130

When the supply of four-cylinder Triumph engines dried up, Morgan switched to the compact Rover V-8 and created the Plus 8. The new engine was an easy fit and didn't alter the Morgan driving feel, just made it possible to enjoy at higher velocities. Alloy wheels, wider track, and a two-inch wheelbase stretch help identify Plus 8s from Plus 4s. Interior trim is more opulent, but construction remains old-world, including wooden underbody pieces. The example pictured is a 1987 model-year Plus 8.

NASH-HEALEY

*I*t's 1949, and budding British automaker Donald Healey is bound for America on the *Queen Elizabeth*, hoping to buy Cadillac V-8s for his latest creation. Also aboard is George Mason, president of Nash-Kelvinator. Mason tells Healey that Caddy's new engine is in short supply, but that Nash's rugged Ambassador six is readily available. By the time they reach New York, a new sports car is born: the Anglo-American Nash-Healey.

A prototype was displayed in Europe within nine short months, and production was underway by 1951 at Healey's small Warwickshire shops, newly expanded for this purpose. The N-H soon made its American debut as a two-seat roadster with slab-sided aluminum body (by Britain's Panelcraft), Healey-designed chassis, and a Nash engine warmed-up by twin carburetors, wilder camshaft, and a special high-compression aluminum cylinder head. Price was Cadillac-costly at $4063, but included leather seats, whitewall tires, and overdrive three-speed manual gearbox.

The N-H quickly proved itself in the most demanding of contemporary European motorsports, but high finishes in the Mille Miglia and at LeMans did nothing for sales at home, which were very low because of the high

price. The N-H was thus revamped for 1952, gaining a stylish new steel body by Italy's Pininfarina, plus, as a running change, a larger Nash six with 10 hp more. But price went some $1800 higher to cover the hefty expense of shipping American powertrains to England, rolling chassis from there to Italy, and completed cars back to the States. Nevertheless, sales rose a bit. Meanwhile, the N-H revisited LeMans, placing third overall and second in the Index of Performance. Nash celebrated for '53 with a stretched-wheelbase LeMans coupe, but priced it at a towering $6399. That year's roadster cost $5908. Once again, though, sales crept up.

Only the coupe returned for '54, with a wrapped rear window and a friendlier $5128 price. But money troubles meant Nash could no longer afford its low-volume sports car, so N-H production was wound down in August, ironically after a final flourish at LeMans (eleventh overall).

For so obviously capable a machine, the Nash-Healey deserved a better fate. It did not die in vain, however, for its disappointing sales led Donald Healey to create a more affordable, Austin-powered sports car, the . . . well, you know.

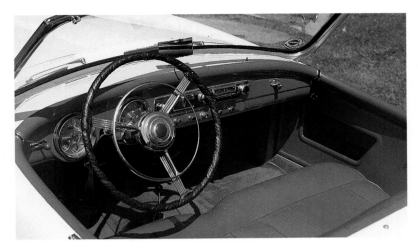

Britisher Donald Healey needed an engine for his new sports car and American automaker Nash needed something its Detroit rivals didn't have. Out of those needs came the Nash-Healey, an intriguingly styled, good-handling two-seater that cost too much to assemble to make much of a splash. The 1951 version had an aluminum body styled by Healey and sold 104 copies. Later N-Hs had steel bodies styled by Pininfarina, as shown here. All had richly appointed interiors. The Nash six gave competitive performance, and actually powered the car to high finishes at LeMans. Production totaled just 506.

Nash-Healey
1951–1954

Wheelbase, in. 102.0

Weight, lbs. 2470

Price $5908

Engine ohv I-6

Displacement liters/cu. in. 4.1/253

Fuel system 2 x 1 bbl. carburetors

Horsepower @ rpm 135 @ 4000

Torque @ rpm 230 @ 2000

Transmission 3-speed manual

Performance

0–60 mph, sec. 11.5

Top speed, mph 102

NISSAN 300ZX TURBO

*B*y 1989, Nissan's proud Z-car felt like a disco-age holdover, and the competition wasn't much better. Mazda's RX-7 Turbo had 200 hp and an identity crisis. The 232-hp Toyota Supra Turbo weighed more than a Cadillac Eldorado. Porsche charged $42,000 for a 944 S2 with a 208-hp four-cylinder, and only big discounts could move the 250-hp Corvette.

Into this fricassee blew the 1990 300ZX, quickly recognized as the benchmark it was. When the 222-hp base model was followed in a few months by the 300-hp Turbo, the birth of the modern, affordable, high-tech sports car was complete.

"A near flawless mix of form, function, and class," raved *Car and Driver*. A one-year evaluation led David E. Davis Jr. of *Automobile* to call the Turbo "as good a high-performance coupe as any company has ever built in any country at any price."

Against the '89 model, the 1990 Z-car had a five-inch-longer wheelbase, but its body—a fluid shape jointly drawn by Nissan's Japan and California studios—was shorter, wider, and lower. A modest rear spoiler, under-grille cooling slots, and a "Twin Turbo" decal subtly differentiated the two-seat

Turbo from the base coupe and 2+2. All used an iron-block, aluminum-head 3.0-liter V-6 with state-of-the-art dual cams and variable-valve timing. To each cylinder bank the Turbo added an oil-cooled turbocharger and an intercooler for lag-free thrust right to the 7000-rpm rev limiter. It also had Nissan's Super HICAS (High Capacity Actively controlled Steering), which turned the rear wheels to provide remarkable transitional stability and surgical steering response. Steering assist was vehicle-speed-dependent, and the driver could adjust the all-independent suspension between touring and sport damping. Balancing this gadgetry was a cockpit of disarming simplicity and comfort, marred only by a frustrating automatic climate system that reset itself each time the car was started.

At $33,000 to start, the '90 Turbo was a terrific performance value, and the car changed only in detail over the years. By 1996, however, the escalating yen had shoved the base price to $43,979, and the bloom was off. The market shifted—to sport-utility vehicles, to lower-tech roadsters, to sport sedans. Nissan didn't import the ZX for '97, and the death of the modern, affordable, high-tech sports car was complete.

Nissan 300ZX Turbo
1990–1996

Wheelbase, in. 96.5

Weight, lbs. 3533

Price $33,000

Engine Twin turbo dohc V-6

Displacement liters/cu. in. 3.0/181

Fuel system Fuel injection

Horsepower @ rpm 300 @ 6400

Torque @ rpm 283 @ 3600

Transmission 5-speed manual

Performance

0–60 mph, sec. 5.6

Top speed, mph 155

Nissan's third—and last—generation Z-car was a stellar blend of speed, style, and technology. It was best represented by the Turbo model, which put two turbochargers on the twincam 3.0-liter V-6 to make 300 hp. The well-sorted suspension and four-wheel steering helped the 300ZX Turbo slice confidently through turns. A sensibly designed cabin added to the enjoyment. But the value of the yen pushed up prices, tastes changed, and by '97, the Z-car was a memory.

PORSCHE 356A

*F*erdinand Porsche was the multitalented genius who engineered Germany's greatest 1930s sports cars, including the supercharged Mercedes SS and all-conquering V-16 racers for Auto Union. He then masterminded a timeless "people's car," the Volkswagen, at the behest of Adolf Hitler. Porsche died in 1950, but not before his son Ferry (Ferdinand Jr.) had begun a sports-car dynasty on the beetle back of the Porsche Type 356.

Conceived as a "sports VW," the 356 started in 1947 as a spartan mid-engine roadster, but was soon made a true rear-engine design by Ferry and longtime Porsche lieutenant Karl Rabe. With Ferry struggling to rebuild his family's war-torn business, the 356 made heavy use of VW components, notably an air-cooled four-cylinder "boxer" engine and all-around torsion-bar suspension with rear swing axles. Styling also paid homage to VW, but was dramatically lower and racier. Like his father, Ferry believed "racing improves the breed," and early competition successes fast bred numerous improvements. By 1954, the 356 was available not only with its original 1100cc engine but as a 1300 and even a

1500 with up to 82 hp. Sales rose yearly, and a move from Gmund, Austria, to larger facilities in Stuttgart helped production keep pace. The total was more than 7600 by 1955, when Porsche turned to the 356A.

As a more thoroughly developed 356, the A shared almost nothing with VW, reflecting Porsche's experience with purpose-built competition cars—and the lucrative U.S. market. The familiar coupe and convertible continued, as did the Speedster, the low-frills low-topped roadster instigated in 1954 by U.S. importer Max Hoffman. Styling also was subtly altered, with one-piece curved windshields notable. There also was more room, revised suspension, and higher performance from 1300 and new 1600 engines. More exciting still was the new 1500GS Carrera, which eschewed pushrods for a detuned 100-hp version of Porsche's twincam racing engine. A 110-hp 1600GS replaced it in 1958.

With constant improvements, granitic construction, and giant-killing prowess on road and track, the 356A cemented Porsche's reputation for sports cars engineered like no other.

The Porsche mystique starts here, with a little inverted bathtub of a sports car that turned defiance of conventional engineering into a virtue. The 356 series lasted from the late 1940s to the mid-1960s. All had an air-cooled flat four-cylinder in the tail and a rear-axle design that made for tricky cornering. But they were quick and extremely well built. Coupes, Cabriolets, and the cut-down-windshield Speedster were offered. This is a 1958 Speedster.

Porsche 356A 1600 Super
1956–1958

Wheelbase, in. 82.7

Weight, lbs. 1900

Price $4000

___

Engine ohv flat-4

Displacement liters/cu. in. 1.6/96.5

Fuel system 2 x 1 bbl. carburetors

Horsepower @ rpm 88 @ 5000

Torque @ rpm 86 @ 3700

Transmission 4-speed manual

Performance

___

0–60 mph, sec. 10.5

Top speed, mph 110

PORSCHE 356C

*T*he 356C was the last, best expression of the four-cylinder formula that fast made Porsche a sports-car power to reckon with. It was also a mere stopgap. By the time the C arrived in mid-1963, Porsche was well along on development of an even more ambitious road car that would prove far longer-lived than the 356.

Not surprisingly then, the C owed much to the 356B, which debuted in late 1959 as an evolution of the well-liked A. The B was easily recognized by its raised front fenders, headlights and bumpers, plus enlarged glass areas. Engines were now exclusively 1600s. The Normal and Super were unchanged from the last A-models at 70 and 88 hp, but a Super 90 model with 102 hp bowed in March 1960. Also new were more efficient cast-aluminum drum brakes and a folding rear seatback newly split for versatility. Improvements for 1961 included premium Koni shocks and a rear "camber compensator." The latter, standard on Super 90s and optional elsewhere, was a transverse leaf spring that helped tame the 356's tendency to snap-throttle oversteer, a trait common to rear-engine cars.

That was especially important to the B-series version of the twincam 356. Logically called Carrera 2, it boasted a wholly different 2.0-liter engine with a smashing 150 hp. Happily, it arrived in spring 1962 with the first all-disc brakes for a production Porsche, borrowed straight from the firm's Formula 1 racers. Minor styling changes graced all '62 Bs, notably twin air intakes in the engine lid and an external fuel filler.

Then came the 356C, discarding domed wheelcovers for flat hubcaps that concealed new all-disc brakes, now a less costly setup devised by Dunlop. Cost also dictated making the camber compensator a $30 option, which some critics found insulting on a $4300 car. The familiar coupe and convertible body styles continued, as did the S and Super 90 engines, but model names were now 1600S and 1600SC. The Carrera 2 also hung on, a rare $7600 example of German engineering at its best.

Then again, every 356 was something special. As *Road & Track* concluded in its 1964 test of a 1600S: "Regardless of what faults one may discover in a Porsche, there is no argument about its comfort, quality and excellent performance." *Herr Doktor* Ferdinand could have asked no higher praise.

Adhering to the Porsche principle, the 356 hung on into its third decade of near-constant improvement but virtually unchanging appearance. The vigorous 356SC was the last and most-advanced expression of the automaker's first production-car series.

Porsche 356SC
1963–1965

Wheelbase, in. 82.7

Weight, lbs. 1970

Price $4300

Engine ohv flat 4-cylinder

Displacement liters/cu. in. 1.6/96.5

Fuel system 2 x 2 bbl. carburetors

Horsepower @ rpm 105 @ 5800

Torque @ rpm 90 @ 3600

Transmission 4-speed manual

Performance

0–60 mph, sec. 13.0

Top speed, mph 105

PORSCHE 904 GTS

*F*or a "customer" racing car of the early 1960s, the 904 GTS was a downright steal at $7500. It was also one of the prettiest of competition cars, so alluring that it almost begged to be run on the street. Some were, but the 904 was no more a daily driver than, say, a Ford GT40.

Only 100 were built, and the few drivers who had the chance discovered that being designed around the semipractical twincam engine of the roadgoing 356 Carrera 2 didn't relieve the 904 from real race-car nuisances: nonexistent sound insulation, no luggage space, poor ventilation, tricky over-the-shoulder visibility.

Mediocre 1961 and '62 seasons in international GT racing may explain why Porsche departed so much from its established engineering practice with the 904. Its body, for example, was fiberglass, not steel or aluminum, and springing was by coils rather than the firm's traditional torsion bars. Actually, the 904's all-around double-wishbone suspension came straight from Porsche's late Formula 1 racer. Also, this was a true mid-engine car, with the flat-four ahead of the rear-axle centerline instead of behind it. That was hardly new to Porsche,

but a five-speed transaxle borrowed from the just-announced roadgoing 911 was. Equally new was the 904's sturdy boxed-rail chassis, to which the body was bonded by Heinkel, the wartime aircraft producer. Styling was by Ferry Porsche's talented son "Butzi" (Ferdinand III), who also penned the 911.

The 904 ended up a bit heavier and less aerodynamic than expected, but had the speed and stamina to be the winner Porsche wanted. Although it failed to finish its 1964 Sebring debut, the 904 snared first and third places in the Targa Florio and third overall at the Nürburgring 1000 Kilometers. Five went to LeMans and finished in the top 12, the highest placing seventh overall. The 904 also conquered the snowy 1965 Monte Carlo Rally, finishing second among 22 survivors of 237 starters.

Alas, rule changes cut short the 904's racing career, and though a few cars were built with milder engines, intriguing plans for a road version were ultimately rendered moot. In that spirit, many 904s have since been fitted with 911 engines—appropriate for a purpose-built racer that seemed to yearn for a place on the street.

Porsche 904 GTS
1964–1965

Wheelbase, in. 90.6

Weight, lbs. 1400

Price $6425

Engine dohc flat-4

Displacement liters/cu. in. 2.0/120

Fuel system 2 x 2 bbl. carburetors

Horsepower @ rpm 180 @ 7800

Torque @ rpm 144 @ 5000

Transmission 5-speed manual

Performance

0–60 mph, sec. 6.4

Top speed, mph 150

The 904 was a dual-purpose sports car that could be—and was—driven on the street. But the true role of this mid-engine two-seat coupe was as a sports-racer. The car pictured was a factory team car and finished first overall in the '64 Targa Florio, second in the '65 Monte Carlo Rally, and third in the GT class at LeMans in '64.

PORSCHE 911

Like "The Fantasticks" on Broadway and TV's *Star Trek*, the Porsche 911 is a 30-year success story with no end in sight. Of course, it was a grand car to start with, but it also proved incredibly adaptable to changing times without losing its fundamental character. Credit the steady honing by Porsche's highly skilled designers and engineers, much of it in the heat of competition. No wonder the 911 has kept packing them in.

The 911 premiered in late 1964 to replace the 356, preserving the formula of a rear-mounted air-cooled boxer engine, torsion-bar suspension, and unitized 2+2 fastback coupe body. The big departures were slightly larger dimensions, new styling by "Butzi" Porsche, a five-speed instead of a four-speed gearbox, and a new 2.0-liter engine with six cylinders, overhead camshafts, and 145 hp. Production didn't hit its stride until mid-1965, by which time the 912 had bowed as a lower-priced companion powered by the 1600SC four-cylinder from the last 356. Two years later came the Targa semi-convertible with removable rear window and a lift-off roof panel above the cockpit. And 1967 also

brought a more potent 911, the 180-hp S. For 1968, Porsche achieved still-broader market coverage by adding a detuned 125-hp 911T, as well as optional "Sportomatic," a three-speed "clutchless" transmission that never was popular.

A 2.3-inch longer wheelbase marked the '69 "B-Series" coupes and Targas, and fuel injection graced the S and mainline 911E. Displacement grew to 2.2 liters for the 1970 "C-Series," which improved low-end pull but, like fuel injection, was chiefly a response to tightening U.S. emissions standards. The 1972 "E-Series" got still more displacement, 2.4 liters, plus another tiny stretch in wheelbase. By that point the S was up to a smashing 210 hp, and even the low-line T had 167. Meanwhile, the 911, like the 356 before it, kept piling up scores of victories in all forms of motorsports, a performance that undoubtedly drew many buyers to the Porsche fold.

But of course, this first decade was only a warm-up. The 911 would become even more suave, sophisticated, and exciting, defying journalistic naysayers, Washington bureaucrats, oil power politics, even time itself.

The sports car that defied time, the 911 was introduced for 1965 as Porsche's successor to the 356 series and is with us today. Like the 356, it put an air-cooled boxer engine in the tail, though now there were six cylinders and overhead cams. The new car also had unitized construction and though its suspension still used torsion bars, it introduced MacPherson struts in front and in back, trailing arms instead of a swing axle. The 911 was roomier and more comfortable than the 356, and initially came in coupe and, as shown on this 1967 model, targa-top body styles. Displacement and power grew continually, and soon Porsches weren't just fast given their engine size, they were just plain fast. The rear weight bias still triggered snap oversteer, and prices never were reasonable. But quality remained high and the 911's image was burnished by lots of racing wins.

Porsche 911
1965–1973

Wheelbase, in. 87.0

Weight, lbs. 2300

Price $6800

Engine ohc flat-6

Displacement liters/cu. in. 2.0/122

Fuel system 2 x 3 bbl. carburetors

Horsepower @ rpm 145 @ 6100

Torque @ rpm 140 @ 4300

Transmission 5-speed manual

Performance

0–60 mph, sec. 9.0

Top speed, mph 130

PORSCHE 914/6

*F*irst impressions can hurt. Although the 914/6 was designed, built, and powered by Porsche, it's not widely regarded as a "real" Porsche. The problem wasn't so much its square, un-Porsche styling—though that didn't help—or its status as Porsche's first mid-engine road car—which *should* have helped. The real problem was that the 914/6 was preceded by a four-cylinder sibling tarred with a half-breed image.

The 914 idea was hatched in the mid-1960s by Volkswagen boss Heinz Nordhoff and Ferry Porsche. Nordhoff wanted a sportier car than his Beetle-based Karmann-Ghia. Porsche wanted a cheaper four-cylinder sports car than the 911-based 912. Deciding that one car might serve two masters, Porsche designed a two-seat Targa-style coupe around the powerplant of a new "big" VW, the 411. Suspension was Porsche 911, modified at the rear to suit the midships format. The Karmann coachworks was tapped to supply the unit steel hulls to both firms.

The 914 thus debuted in Europe late in 1969 under a new "VW-Porsche" banner as the product of a jointly held marketing company. It even wore confusing "VW-Porsche" badging that reinforced the muddled image. In March 1970, the VW-powered sports car came to the United States, where it bore only a Porsche badge.

No matter. As marque authority Karl Ludvigsen wrote, the 914 was "both VW and Porsche and neither VW *nor* Porsche." Though it tempted with a well-planned cockpit, surprising luggage space, open-air appeal, and mid-engine mystique, its performance was tame and its price stiff—initially $3495 in the U.S.

A whopping $2600 more bought the 914/6, which arrived during 1970 with a genuine Porsche flat-six (the 125-hp 911T engine), plus 911S-type alloy wheels, fatter tires, larger brakes, and deluxe trim. Alas, it proved even harder to sell than the four-cylinder job, and was quietly canned after model-year '72. With it went the "916," a planned fixed-top evolution with bulging wheel arches, color-keyed bumpers, deep front air dam, and a 190-hp 2.4-liter six projected to go 0–60 mph in under seven seconds. Porsche built 20 prototypes of this would-be Ferrari Dino challenger before deciding it made no financial sense. Porsche soon felt likewise about the 914, and belatedly put it to rest in 1976.

Though a relative failure, the 914 still has fans today. Naturally, the 914/6 is the most desired model by far, but what a pity not even its extra "Porsche-ness" could overcome first impressions.

Not every Porsche sports car is a long-lived success. The 914 was the result of a star-crossed liaison between Volkswagen and Porsche. It came with an inline four-cylinder VW engine or as the 914/6 with a twincam 2.0-liter Porsche flat-six and wider tires. The latter was a capable car but was never accepted as a full-fledged Porsche and died after 3351 were built (compared to 78,643 "914/4s"). Both versions used a removable targa-top and put the engine behind the seats. Engine access was poor (left), but the layout allowed for cargo compartments front and rear (below).

Porsche 914/6
1970–1972

Wheelbase, in. 96.4

Weight, lbs. 2200

Price $6100

Engine dohc flat-6

Displacement liters/cu. in. 2.0/122

Fuel system 2 x 3 bbl. carburetors

Horsepower @ rpm 125 @ 5800

Torque @ rpm 131 @ 4200

Transmission 5-speed manual

Performance

0–60 mph, sec. 8.7

Top speed, mph 123

PORSCHE TURBO CARRERA

*T*he first roadgoing 911 Turbo flew against everything deemed politically correct for a late-1970s automobile. But oh, how it flew! Acceleration felt like being aboard a jet on takeoff, "when you're forced into the seat by some mysterious and remote power," said Britain's *Motor. Car and Driver* deemed the Turbo "a Panzer among Porsches, a street racer that will guarantee you a place at the top of the pecking order [like] no Ferrari or Lamborghini can."

Porsche began experimenting with exhaust-boosted power in the late '60s for the mighty turbocharged 917s that dominated Can-Am racing in the early '70s. Soon, engineers under company veteran Dr. Ernst Fuhrmann devised a "blown" competition 911, the RSR Turbo, which extracted 333 hp from just 2.1 liters. They also worked on a road version that became so different from ordinary 911s as to merit its own model number, 930. It reached Europe in 1975 as the 911 Turbo and came to America as the 1976-model Turbo Carrera.

The 930 benefitted from all the 911's considered changes for 1974–75, including U.S.-mandated "safety bumpers" so artfully wrought as to look as if they'd always been there. But where 911s had progressed to 2.7-liter engines, the Turbo got a 3.0 for better torque and off-boost performance. Torque was in fact so prodigious that a four-speed gearbox was deemed sufficient instead of the 911's five-speed.

More readily apparent were a racing-derived "whale tail" spoiler and wider rear wheels within menacingly bulged openings. Stiffer damping also helped cope with the Turbo's extra power. Adjustable Koni shocks were among the few factory options because Porsche loaded the 930 with all manner of standard "extras," including air conditioning, leather, and power windows. Still, this was a barely tamed beast that could scare even professional drivers with its sudden oversteer and "omigod!" thrust. If you mastered it, you were king—as you almost needed to be to own one.

All of which made it one of the most desired cars on the planet. Although Porsche has since produced faster, more sophisticated 911 Turbos, this is the original, the one that taunted drivers and mocked a post–energy crisis world.

Porsche Turbo Carrera
1976–1977

Wheelbase, in. 89.4

Weight, lbs. 2785

Price $26,000

Engine Turbo ohc flat-6

Displacement liters/cu. in. 3.0/183

Fuel system Fuel injection

Horsepower @ rpm 234 @ 5500

Torque @ rpm 246 @ 5000

Transmission 4-speed manual

Performance

0–60 mph, sec. 4.9

Top speed, mph 156

While rivals suffered post–energy crisis indecision, Porsche unleashed one of the first turbocharged road cars, the tempestuous and sometimes scary Turbo Carrera. Its 3.0 liter was larger than the flat-six in other 911 models and had enough turbo lag to make snap oversteer a constant threat in turns. But it also turned the 911 into a genuine supercar. The chassis was heavily reengineered to cope, while wider back tires, flared rear fenders, and a trademark whale tail spoiler gave it a look worthy of its bad attitude. Worldwide Turbo Carrera production was 2873.

PORSCHE 911 CABRIOLET

*S*urprise and delight greeted the new Porsche unveiled at the 1982 Geneva auto show: delight at the firm's first true convertible since the last 356 cabriolet of 17 years earlier, and surprise that it was not an open-air version of the newer front-engine 924 or 928. Some observers took that soft-top 911SC as evidence that the rear-engine Porsche would not soon go the way of the dodo, as was then being predicted. Boy, were they right.

The ageless 911 had received a strong new lease on life with the upgrade to SC specifications for 1978. Chief among the changes was a still-further enlarged flat-six, now essentially an "unblown" version of the 3.0-liter Turbo Carrera engine. U.S. models added a catalytic converter, which, combined with the extra displacement, improved driveability and performance despite the tightening emissions limits. Standard front and rear anti-roll bars were another first for a 911, but the Sportomatic "clutchless" manual transmission was gone. By the time the Cabrio debuted, all 911s, coupes and Targas alike, had been spruced up with standard air conditioning, power windows, leather seats, even headlight washers.

The Cabrio had all these, too, though its manual top with a zip-out plastic rear window seemed rather mean for the costliest non-turbo 911—initially $34,450 in the United States. At least it did benefit performance by holding weight to SC-coupe level. And typical of Porsche, the top was fully lined for comfort and quiet, as well as easy to operate. Tellingly, the basic 911 structure proved stout enough that little strengthening was needed to achieve acceptable rigidity in the convertible, which evidenced nary a rattle from body or roof.

For 1984, the Cabrio and other SCs took on the hallowed Carrera name, as well as a still-further enlarged engine, now 3.2 liters. U.S. horses went from 172 to 200, then to 214 for 1987. Fortunately, brakes were enlarged, too. For boulevard bragging, Porsche briefly offered a "Turbo Look" option that made any 911 into the spitting image of the awesome 930—provided you came up with (gulp) an extra $25,000.

The 911 Cabrio sold well enough to outlive the original Targa body style. It's with us still, and better than ever. That's no surprise. After all, what other sports car marries two such timeless ideas as 911 and convertible?

Porsche 911 Carrera Cabriolet
1982–1988

Wheelbase, in. 89.4

Weight, lbs. 2760

Price $51,250

Engine ohc flat-6

Displacement liters/cu. in. 3.2/193

Fuel system Fuel injection

Horsepower @ rpm 214 @ 5900

Torque @ rpm 195 @ 4800

Transmission 5-speed manual

Performance

0–60 mph, sec. 7.0

Top speed, mph 130

Porsche continued to hone its 911 range, upgrading it to SC specs and a standard 3.0-liter flat-six for 1978. This model was the basis for the firm's first true convertible since the 356C of 1965. It was introduced for 1982 with all the luxury amenities well-heeled 911 buyers had come to expect, though use of a manual rather than automatic folding roof seemed at odds with its price. Still, the fully lined top was well engineered and no convertible was more structurally sound than the 911 Cabrio. This 1987 model bears the Carrera name and 3.2-liter engine adopted by 911s in 1984. One constant was the Porsche crest, first sketched by Ferry Porsche on a napkin in 1952.

PORSCH 924 TURBO

A friend of ours once remarked that if you turbocharge a bad car, you get a bad turbocharged car. While the short-lived 924 Turbo was hardly a bad car, more was expected from a Porsche than this one generally delivered.

The Turbo arrived some four years after the 924, which was introduced in 1975 (for '77 in the U.S.) as a new "budget" Porsche to replace the 914. As with that mid-engine car, Volkswagen was the impetus, and Porsche again did the engineering around off-the-shelf components. Then VW backed out but this time, Porsche took things over entirely. There was no question of blurred identity, although production was entrusted to VW's Audi branch. The result was the first Porsche with a water-cooled front-mounted inline engine to reach production, although the 924 was actually designed *after* the like-formatted V-8-powered 928, which bowed during 1977.

The new entry-level Porsche was a shapely 2+2 coupe with a smooth hidden-headlamp nose, lift-up "glassback," and a 2.0-liter Audi four driving through a thin, flexible propshaft to a four-speed rear transaxle. An optional three-speed automatic was added in '76, and a five-speed manual option arrived for 1978. The 924 was a fine handler thanks to an all-independent suspension and a near-50/50 weight balance, but critics carped about its off-center steering wheel, odd conical gauge lenses, sub-Porsche workmanship, tepid performance and—especially—the loud, throbby engine.

Porsche took the criticism to heart with the 924 Turbo, which blew in wearing four nasal air slots and a functioning hood duct, unique alloy wheels, and front/rear spoilers. Adding a turbocharger and a new Porsche-designed cylinder head upped horsepower from 95–110 in U.S. form to a more exciting 143. Even better, the five-speed was now standard for all 924s, and Porsche itself built the Turbo cars. With all this, Britain's *Autocar* magazine hailed the blown 924 as "another *real* Porsche." Alas, the engine remained a buzzbox and the ride was even lumpier, thanks to a firmed-up chassis and higher-performance tires. Worse, U.S. price crept up to around $20,000, more than double that of the first non-turbo model.

But just as the 356 begat the superior 911, the 924 Turbo led to the even better 944. The 944 replaced the Turbo after 1981, though a steadily improved non-turbo 924 would continue as Porsche's price-leader through 1988. In all, the 924 Turbo was a good sports car. It just wasn't a great Porsche.

To field a reasonably priced entry-level model, Porsche again risked association with a less-prestigious automaker, this time Audi. The 924 debuted in Europe for 1975 as the first production Porsche with a water-cooled front engine. Audi built both the four-cylinder and the smooth 2+2 coupe, which handled well but was noisy, stiff, and overpriced for the modest performance. It wasn't accepted as a true Porsche until the Turbo version of 1979. It was built entirely by Porsche and its turbocharged 2.0-liter four (below) made a respectable 143 hp. The cabin was sporty, but materials were not to Porsche standards.

Porsche 924 Turbo
1979–1981

Wheelbase, in. 94.5

Weight, lbs. 2835

Price $21,000

Engine Turbo ohc I-4

Displacement liters/cu. in. 2.0/122

Fuel system Fuel injection

Horsepower @ rpm 143 @ 5000

Torque @ rpm 147 @ 3000

Transmission 5-speed manual

Performance

0–60 mph, sec. 7.7

Top speed, mph 132

PORSCHE 928

When is a GT like a sports car? When it's a Porsche 928. Think of it as a German Corvette: big, brawny, and quick, relaxed on straights, athletic on curves, voiced by a burble that could come only from a V-8.

Yet somehow, it didn't quite work out. Despite patient polishing over nearly 20 years, the 928 suffered the same sort of "Porsche identity crisis" that plagued its four-cylinder kid brother, the 924. That was cruel, because the 928 actually was the first "all-Porsche Porsche" with no ties to the marque's humble Volkswagen origins.

By the time the 928 arrived in 1977, the 911 had long fixed "Porsche" as meaning a compact 2+2 with an air-cooled rear-mounted flat-six. How could this heavy hatchback coupe compare? In truth, it didn't have to. Judged on its own terms, the 928 was genuine Porsche: logical in every way, immensely capable, and solid as the Brandenburg Gate. It just wasn't accepted as a 911 replacement, which had been Porsche's original goal.

The 928 changed only in detail over the years, so it always had a water-cooled overhead-cam all-aluminum V-8, manual or automatic rear transaxle, novel "Weissach" rear suspension with self-correcting toe control, and a sensible tilt steering wheel/instrument cluster assembly. The ini-

tial 218-hp 4.5-liter V-8 became a 234-hp 4.7 for 1983. Two years later, Porsche doubled cams to create a 5.0-liter dohc dynamo with 288 hp, which then swelled to 316 hp for 1987's modestly facelifted "S4" (Series 4). That designation vanished for 1990, but standard dual air bags arrived and emissions-legal power rose once more, reaching 326. The following year introduced the GT tag for manual-shift 928s, while S4 returned on automatic models. The final development was 1993's 5.4-liter GTS with a mighty 345 hp, smoothed-out styling, and 5.5-second 0–60-mph capability.

Along the way, the 928 shed "op-art" checked upholstery fabric, gained anti-lock control for its big all-disc brakes, and became more aerodynamically efficient. It was never cheap—excellence never is—but neither was it exorbitantly priced for a carefully crafted "executive express" able to span continents with contemptuous ease.

The 928 was dropped after 1995 as irrelevant to Porsche's future—ironic considering how it began *as* Porsche's future. Yet this was, as *Road & Track* once declared, "one of the world's finest *gran turismos*. . . . Also, one of the most underrated. And unappreciated." Perhaps in death, the 928 will finally be prized as the superb performance car it always was.

Porsche 928 GTS
1993–1995

Wheelbase, in. 98.4

Weight, lbs. 3600

Price $81,000

Engine dohc V-8

Displacement liters/cu. in. 5.4/329

Fuel system Fuel injection

Horsepower @ rpm 345 @ 5700

Torque @ rpm 369 @ 4250

Transmission 5-speed manual

Performance

0–60 mph, sec. 5.5

Top speed, mph 171

Anyone who passed on Porsche's first liquid-cooled, front-engine model because it didn't fit the marque's image or wasn't as flashy as a Ferrari missed one of the world's fastest and best-engineered sporting automobiles. Highlights of the 928 series included an all-alloy V-8 linked to a rear transaxle, a suspension of unsurpassed capability, and rock-solid workmanship. Shown is the ultimate iteration, the quad-cam, 345-hp GTS introduced for 1993. Apathy killed the 928 after 1995.

PORSCHE 944S2

As the 944 improved on the 924, the S2 was a better 944. That's Porsche's way: Start with an outstanding basic design, then sweat the details.

There was nothing about the 924 that a new engine wouldn't fix. The 944 fixed it, bowing in 1982 with an all-Porsche slant-four. Displacing 2.5 liters, it was basically half of the 928's V-8, refined with vibration-damping balance shafts. Initial U.S. horsepower was 147, outmuscling even the 924 Turbo, and Porsche kept it under control with standard all-disc brakes and a suitably beefed-up chassis. With that, the 944 was quicker than the 924 Turbo, stickier in corners—and vastly easier on the ears. It also was more arresting to the eyes, thanks to blistered fenders and other styling tweaks. Critics cheered and buyers lined up. Finally, the front-engine four-cylinder Porsche had made good.

But good is seldom enough for Porsche, so in 1986 it introduced the 944 Turbo, with functional aero-body enhancements, a rousing 217 hp, and 6.1-second 0–60 mph ability. Then, to fill a price gap between models, Porsche conjured the 944S, with a new 16-valve cylinder head and other improvements that gave more linear power

delivery than the Turbo, yet nearly as much go from its 188 hp. Over the next two years, Porsche made anti-lock brakes and dual air bags available on all 944s.

Unfortunately, rising prices were hurting sales, and Porsche was in trouble by 1989, though you couldn't tell from that year's '44s. A bigger-bore 2.7-liter engine gave the base car 162 hp, while the Turbo went to 247 via a bigger blower. Then there was the new S2, which looked like the Turbo but packed a thumping 3.0-liter twincam with 208 hp. Beyond extra size, the engine was fully updated. The S2 could run on regular gas, yet scamper like the Turbos of just a few years before. *Motor Trend* judged it "quicker in the real world in all but the most demanding circumstances." The editors also praised its "Porsche-ness," that indefinable quality "that makes the driving experience somehow more satisfying. . . ." As if all that weren't enough, Porsche also had a new S2 cabriolet. It was pricey (nearly $53,000), but solid, draft-free, and eminently desirable.

Yet for all its goodness, the S2 was short-lived. The reason was still *another* improvement on the front four-cylinder theme, the svelte 968.

Porsche 944S2
1989–1990

Wheelbase, in. 94.5

Weight, lbs. 2932

Price $46,000

Engine dohc I-4

Displacement liters/cu. in. 3.0/183

Fuel system Fuel injection

Horsepower @ rpm 208 @ 5800

Torque @ rpm 207 @ 4100

Transmission 5-speed manual

Performance

0–60 mph, sec. 6.2

Top speed, mph 145

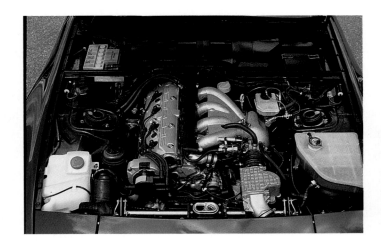

Porsche's solution to the less-than-inspiring 924 was the 944. It bowed for 1982 with a beefed-up chassis, blistered fenders, new nose, and a lot more presence. The four-cylinder engine was larger and stronger, culminating in the S2's 208-hp twin-cam 3.0 liter. A 944 cabriolet bowed in 1988. In 1987, the 944 Turbo became the first car sold in the U.S. with dual air bags.

PORSCHE 959

*I*n the mid-1980s, when international authorities devised Group B racing for "factory experimental" cars, Porsche devised a *panzerwagen*. Although Group B was cut short because of tragic accidents, the 959 remains a towering technical achievement and one of the most desirable cars ever built.

Looking like a 911 coupe on steroids, the 959's steel central body bulged with functional aerodynamic panels rendered in lightweight Kevlar and other high-tech materials. Massive tires wrapped around huge anti-lock disc brakes. All four wheels were powered by a special short-stroke 2.8-liter horizontally opposed six with dual turbochargers operating sequentially, plus water-cooled heads, titanium connecting rods, and other premium features. The drive system employed a six-speed gearbox with extra-low first gear (allegedly for "off-road" use) and a front differential with a multi-plate hydraulic clutch acting as a differential; the normal rear diff was a locking limited-slip type. Front/rear torque apportioning was computer-controlled or followed one of four driver-selected programs: "Traction" (both ends locked for maximum pull), "Ice" (50/50), "Wet" (40/60), and "Dry" (40/60, to 20/80 in hard acceleration). Suspension departed from 911 tra-

dition with double wishbones and twin coil-over shocks all-around. The shocks, also computer-controlled, offered soft, firm, and automatic damping modes, plus three ride heights.

The 959 was sold in fairly plush "Comfort" form and as a detrimmed Sport weighing 110–130 lbs less. Both offered over 190 mph, 0–60 in about four seconds, and stupendous handling. A competition version, the 961, proved itself by winning the punishing Paris-Dakar Rally in 1984 and '86.

As a costly technical showcase with deliberately limited production, the 959 was too specialized to warrant certification for U.S. sale—which only made Americans want it more. A few did come Stateside, but most stayed in Europe. Porsche built just 230 examples of the largely handcrafted car, including prototypes and 961s.

Happily, the 959 was more than a short-lived racer for the road. As British journalist Mel Nichols wrote: "No car has ever affected me as deeply as this one . . . I love it most because it gives so much and asks for so little. . . .[Yet] it is the tip of an iceberg: Other Porsches will gain the 959's technology and degrees of its prowess." He was right, and today's 911 Carrera 4 and 911 Turbo prove it.

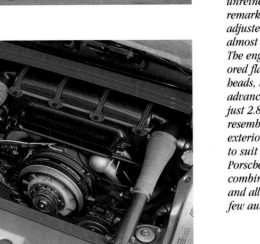

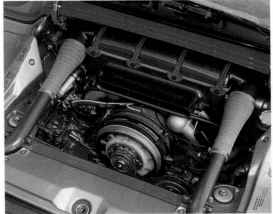

Porsche 959
1987–1988

Wheelbase, in. 89.4

Weight, lbs. 3088

Price $180,000

Engine Twin-turbo dohc flat-6

Displacement liters/cu. in. 2.8/174

Fuel system Fuel injection

Horsepower @ rpm 450 @ 6500

Torque @ rpm 369 @ 5500

Transmission 6-speed manual

Performance

0–60 mph, sec. 3.7

Top speed, mph 190

The 959 was a towering technological achievement built by Porsche as a racing car. Its competition series disbanded before it could run, and the world was left with a roadgoing sports car of fabled performance. Porsche's engineering obsession was unreined for this one. It started with a remarkable all-wheel-drive system that adjusted the distribution of power to suit almost every driving situation imaginable. The engine employed Porsche's time-honored flat-six layout, but used water-cooled heads, two turbochargers, and other advanced features to pump 450 hp from just 2.8 liters. Similarly, the cabin and body resembled those of the familiar 911, but the exterior was ducted, spoiled, and widened to suit the elevated needs of the 959. Porsche built just 230 of these cars, which combined levels of acceleration, top speed, and all-around control rivaled by precious few automobiles in history.

PORSCHE CARRERA 4

Many people seem attracted to Porsches simply because Porsche goes its own way, succeeding brilliantly with unique solutions to automotive problems. The 911 proves the point. Against all odds, its unique character survived countless changes, a tribute to Porsche's skill and persistence with a basic design that some said was outmoded even when new.

The 911 entered its second quarter-century in 1989 with a stem-to-stern overhaul developed within Porsche as Project 964. Styling was little changed—to the undoubted relief of 911 fans—but subtly re-shaped front and rear ends improved aerodynamics, and the inner structure was so fully redesigned (mainly for easier manufacturing) as to have little in common with earlier models. The chassis was mod-ernized with all-around coil-over shocks, front wishbones, and rear semitrailing arms, plus the first power steering in 911 history. Last but not least, the evergreen air-cooled flat-six expanded to 3.6 liters and a healthy 247 hp in U.S. trim.

The centerpiece of Project 964 was the "poor man's 959," the

Carrera 4. The "4" denoted a standard four-wheel-drive system that was vastly simpler than the 959's, yet more responsive. Torque was normally split 31 percent front/69 percent rear, but the system's elec-tronics would instantly vary that through selective use of electrohy-draulic clutches in center and rear differentials. Anti-lock brakes were integral to the package, and both diffs could be locked for extra grip on ice or snow. All this for a third the price of a 959.

Although the "C4" couldn't be 959-hot, it was very fast. *Car and Driver* clocked a standing quarter-mile of 13.2 seconds at 102 mph. As for handling, the C4 was a revelation for a street 911. In *C/D*'s view, Porsche, "gained so much balance with the Carrera 4 that we no longer consider [the rear-drive 911 Turbo] a class contender among high-dollar sports cars."

Porsche hadn't forgotten purists, of course, so a rear-drive version, the Carrera 2, bowed for 1990. With it came "Tiptronic," a four-speed automatic transmission that could be shifted like a manual, yet was smart enough to stay in the "right" gear even if the driver wasn't.

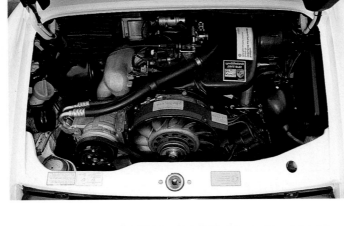

Its unmistakable shape was unaltered, but the new 911 for 1989 got reshaped front and rear ends, as well as a fully revamped understructure. The flat-six grew to 3.6 liters and now powered all the tires via Porsche's new four-wheel-drive system. It was standard on the aptly named Carrera 4 and finally eradicated any hint of tail-happy cornering. A rear-drive Carrera 2 companion bowed for 1990. Both featured a rear spoiler/grille that automatically flipped up at 50 mph to aid engine cooling and provide down-force, then folded back down at 6 mph.

Porsche Carrera 4
1989–1994

Wheelbase, in. 89.5

Weight, lbs. 3200

Price $69,500

Engine ohc flat-6

Displacement liters/cu. in. 3.6/220

Fuel system Fuel injection

Horsepower @ rpm 247 @ 6100

Torque @ rpm 228 @ 4800

Transmission 5-speed manual

Performance

0–60 mph, sec. 5.1

Top speed, mph 162

PORSCHE 968

*I*t's tempting to dismiss the 968 as a facelifted 944, but things are never that simple with Porsches. Fact is, the 968 was the last and finest of an admirable breed.

Announced for 1992, the 968 followed Porsche tradition by keeping the best of its predecessor and improving the rest. There was no Turbo version this time, just a well-equipped coupe and cabriolet, again with all-independent suspension and rear transaxle. Lay-back headlamps in a reshaped nose provided distinction from the 944 and a family kinship with the big 928.

Cost considerations mandated use of the 944S2's 3.0-liter four-cylinder, but horsepower swelled by 28 via tight 11:1 compression and freer-flow exhaust. Even with dual cams and a new variable-valve-timing system, a jumbo four seemed a bit unsophisticated for Porsche. But it was highly effective. The 968 engine boasted the most torque of any non-turbo 3.0 liter in the world. A new six-speed gearbox helped put it to the ground more flexibly than the previous five-speed, and Porsche's innovative "Tiptronic" transmission (borrowed from the 911) gave the four-cylinder line its first automatic option since 1989.

The convertible arguably looked better than the closed car, and like the S2 convertible, the 968 cabrio was a coupe conversion completed between Audi and a German branch of American Sunroof Corporation. Rear-seat space was token and the trunk was barely taller than a pizza, but the open 968 was impressively rigid on rough roads and virtually draft-free at any speed.

Speaking of speed, the 968 was the fastest non-racing four-cylinder Porsche ever, with 0–60 mph times of well under six seconds. Handling? Simply superb, what with a body-tugging skidpad mark of near 0.95g. But then, this *was* a Porsche. Unfortunately, it was priced like one. But, as *Car and Driver* declared: ". . . Years from now, [we] will still be able to call up accurate memories of how this car *went*. In that, if not [test numbers] or on the bottom line of price versus performance, the 968 is a winner. . . ."

Slow sales suggested otherwise. Underneath it all, the 968 was a near 20-year-old design. Besides, Porsche was preparing a new entry-level car, the Boxster. The 968 disappeared after 1995, but don't bet against its future as a collector car.

Porsche 968 Cabriolet
1992–1995

Wheelbase, in. 94.5

Weight, lbs. 3240

Price $52,200

Engine dohc I-4

Displacement liters/cu. in. 3.0/183

Fuel system Fuel injection

Horsepower @ rpm 236 @ 6200

Torque @ rpm 225 @ 4100

Transmission 6-speed manual

Performance

0–60 mph, sec. 5.9

Top speed, mph 153

Porsche's ultimate refinement of its entry-level front-engine design was the 968. Superb road manners, enticing coupe and convertible styling, and a surprisingly strong 3.0-liter four-cylinder engine won it deserved credibility. Production totaled 19,120 worldwide.

PORSCHE 911 TURBO

Rev it to 4500 rpm and dump the clutch. Four tires claw, and it launches. The orange needle springs around the tachometer face, but too much is happening out the windshield to fix on its arrival at the suddenly inadequate 6600-rpm redline, so you shift by ear. The car is so stable that your principal task becomes snatching a new gear each few seconds. After things settle down you glance behind the seat. Change has been sucked from your pocket.

This is "the most obscenely fast and sophisticated Porsche since Weissach loosed upon civilized society the all-wheel-drive 959 nine years ago," says *Car and Driver*. To *Road & Track*, it's nothing less than "the Porsche of Porsches."

It's the 911 Turbo, the ultimate incarnation of the latest version of the oldest Porsche. It belongs to the 993 series, the revised 911 Carerra line that bowed for 1995 with laid-back headlamps, gentle fender flares, and a tapered new tail. A new double-wishbone rear suspension continued the battle against snap oversteer. And the 3.6-liter boxer six now spun 270 hp through a new six-speed gearbox. It pushed the $66,000 rear-drive Carrera 2 to 60 mph in 4.7 seconds and on up to 162 mph.

The second-generation all-wheel-drive Carrera 4 got a new viscous clutch that reapportioned power (up to 39 percent) to the front wheels only when traction demanded. It worked better than the original C4's computer-controlled system, and weighed half as much. The '95 C4 debuted at $72,000, did 0–60 in 4.9 seconds, and hit 161 mph.

For 1996, Porsche pulled the trigger on the new Turbo. A reshaped whale tail complimented still-wider rear fenders, and all-wheel drive now served the most-powerful U.S.-legal production Porsche ever. Like the previous Turbo, it had an all-aluminum two-valve 3.6, but instead of one turbocharger, it had two smaller blowers for more progressive boost. There was higher compression, smarter engine-management electronics, an extra gear, and unprecedented performance, including 0.95g cornering.

No $100,000 car is a "good value," but nothing short of a Ferrari F50, which costs about five times as much, or the McClaren F1, at eight times the price, can touch the 911 Turbo. And the Porsche carries four passengers and 7.5 cubic feet of luggage in all-weather confidence. Just leave your loose change at home.

Porsche 911 Turbo
1996–

Wheelbase, in. 89.4

Weight, lbs. 3362

Price $106,465

Engine Twin turbo ohc flat-6

Displacement liters/cu. in. 3.6/220

Fuel system Fuel injection

Horsepower @ rpm 400 @ 5750

Torque @ rpm 400 @ 4500

Transmission 6-speed manual

Performance

0–60 mph, sec. 3.7

Top speed, mph 176

Porsche's latest 911 debuted for 1995 with laid-back head-lamps, flared fenders, and a tapered tail. The Turbo version combines the best of Porsche to create an all-wheel-drive, dual-blower coupe of stupendous performance. No supercar matches its blend of utility, quality, and reliability and few road cars ever made are as fast.

PORSCHE BOXSTER

*P*orsche seldom bothers to build concept cars, never mind sell them, so the Boxster is quite special apart from being a much-anticipated new open Porsche. For one thing, its show-car styling, unveiled at Detroit '93, has survived to production nearly intact. And beautiful it is, with echoes of the great 1950s RSK and 550 Spyders. The Boxster also pays homage to the very first Porsche, the 356/1 prototype, in having a true mid-engine layout. Yet for all its "history," this is a thoroughly modern marvel sharing no parts with any Porsche past or present—though it will share some with the next 911.

The production car is somewhat longer, wider, and taller than the Boxster concept—about 911-size, in fact. The increases were made to provide sufficient accident crush space, cargo room (via trunks front and rear), and storage for the power soft top, which disappears beneath a hinged cover. Safety and cost also dictated a body/chassis of steel rather than any exotic materials.

The all-aluminum flat-six is no surprise coming from Porsche, but the Boxster's is a twincam *water-cooled* design with new "Varioram" induc-

tion that helps extract a 201 hp from just 2.5 liters. For packaging and refinement, the engine is effectively encapsulated, with no access from above save two service ports. Transmissions comprise a six-speed manual or a new five-speed version of Porsche's "Tiptronic" auto/manual.

Suspension is independent by compact coil-sprung struts. Other features include anti-lock disc brakes, dual air bags, and a reinforced windshield frame strong enough for rollover protection. Among the few options are a cockpit "wind blocker," traction control, and a 55-lb aluminum hardtop.

How does it go? Wonderfully. "At 5200 rpm, [the engine] delivers a passionate howl and hurls the car forward toward an even deeper wail at 6000," reported *Car and Driver*: "It is the sound of a fanatically eager engine . . . The suspension is taut, but it still delivers a quiet and compliant ride." And get this: "You can dive into a tight second-gear corner, back off, even brake if you like, and the Boxster doesn't deviate off line." Overall, *C/D* judged the Boxster "the most dynamic and exciting of the new-generation of two-seat roadsters." A new Porsche legend? Sounds like it.

As the new roadsters from BMW and Mercedes reflected their makers' traditions, the mid-engine Boxster mirrored Porsche's unconventional spirit. It was the most serious performance sports car of the bunch, using its midships layout to create a track-ready feel. The styling was adventurous inside and out, and the designers encapsulated the liquid-cooled flat-six behind the two-seat cockpit. A removable windblocker panel bridged the padded magnesium roll bars.

Porsche Boxster
1997–

Wheelbase, in. 95.1

Weight, lbs. 2755

Price $39,980

Engine dohc flat-6

Displacement liters/cu. in. 2.5/151

Fuel system Fuel injection

Horsepower @ rpm 201 @ 6000

Torque @ rpm 181 @ 4500

Transmission 6-speed manual

Performance

0–60 mph, sec. 6.7

Top speed, mph 149

SHELBY GT-350

*R*eal sports cars are not gilded versions of passenger coupes, but sometimes, sports cars are as sports cars do.

When Carroll Shelby reworked a 1965 Ford Mustang to within an inch of its ponycar life, the result was a howling, hard-riding, two-seat fastback that beat the pants off a passel of "authentic" sports cars. "It is . . . certainly the most sporting street machine we have driven in a long while, and anyone who tells you it isn't a genuine sports car is nuts," said *Car and Driver* in its very first test of the Shelby GT-350.

With Mustang a sales sensation after its April 1964 debut, Ford chief Lee Iacocca sought some performance credibility by going Corvette-hunting in Sports Car Club of America B-production racing. He recruited Shelby, who had just stuffed the British A.C. Ace with Ford power to create the Cobra.

Shelby's team worked out of a small shop in Venice, California. Ford shipped over white fastback Mustangs fitted with the "Hi-Performance" 289 V-8, four-speed gearbox, front discs, and Ford Galaxie drum brakes and rear axle in place of the stock Mustang's lighter Falcon pieces. Shelby-American stiffened the structure, supplemented the suspension, reworked the steering, and fitted 15 x 6-inch wheels with Goodyear Blue Dot high-

speed tires. It added 35 hp with an aluminum manifold and larger carb, slapped on side-exit dual exhausts, and installed a 4.11:1 locking differential. All cars got a scooped fiberglass hood, and most had extra-cost blue racing stripes. By omitting the rear seat, GT-350s could race as sports cars rather than sedans. Competition "R" models had no interior trim and got a blueprinted Cobra racing 289, fiberglass nose valance with cooling ducts, plexiglas side windows, 34-gallon gas tank, and 15 x 7 magnesium wheels.

Priced at $4547—$1000 below a Corvette—the GT-350 got rave reviews, while the $5950 R-model cleaned up in B-production, winning the 1965 national championship and four of five regional titles. The same cars won again in '66 and in '67.

The 1966 GT-350s got plexiglas rear quarter windows, bodyside air scoops, and eventually came in more colors. They had a backseat, tamer suspension and steering, and offered the locking diff as an option—along with automatic transmission. Shelby even built about 1000 gold-striped GT-350H models for the Hertz rental fleet. Shelby Mustangs grew increasingly softer after '66, and were eventually absorbed into regular Ford production, leaving the original editions as exemplary exceptions to the sports-car rule.

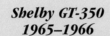

Shelby GT-350
1965–1966

Wheelbase, in. 108.0

Weight, lbs. 2850

Price $4500

Engine ohv V-8

Displacement liters/cu. in. 4.7/289

Fuel system 1 x 4 bbl. carburetor

Horsepower @ rpm 306 @ 6000

Torque @ rpm 329 @ 4200

Transmission 4-speed manual

Performance

0–60 mph, sec. 6.5

Top speed, mph 126

A sports car in ponycar clothing, the GT-350 was a race winner and an American classic. Carroll Shelby turned the underpowered, soft-handling Mustang into a Corvette-hungry production-class racer. Street GT-350s like the 1965 model pictured were only slightly less vicious than the GT-350R race cars. Both used a Mustang chassis with a beefed-up suspension and structural enhancements. They shared Ford's 289 V-8, but with modifications that gave street cars 306 hp and racers about 360. A wood-rimmed wheel, extra gauge pod, wide seat belts, and side-exit exhausts were standard. Substituting a spare-tire shelf for the rear seat allowed GT-350s to race as sports cars. A roll bar was not standard on street versions.

SUNBEAM TIGER

*S*helby's A.C. Cobra wasn't the only British sports car to benefit from Ford V-8 power. The Sunbeam Tiger boasted genuine Carroll Shelby involvement, and could be regarded as a sort of "Cobra junior."

Sunbeam was the sportiest of several English brands controlled by Britain's Rootes Group. Sunbeam had run Grand Prix events and Indianapolis and built sporting road cars before the Rootes takeover in 1935. Rootes marketed touring cars under the Sunbeam-Talbot badge, but not until the '50s did the name appear on a sports car, the Sunbeam Alpine. Seeking more performance for this trusty if timidly styled four-cylinder roadster, Rootes contracted with Shelby for a prototype with Ford small-block power. Dubbed the Tiger—after Sunbeam's 1928 land-speed-record car—it debuted at the 1964 New York Auto Show and soon went into production in England.

Visually similar to the concurrent Alpine, the Tiger shared the Cobra's 260-cid Ford V-8, but in milder tune than that 260-hp bomb. Still, its 164 hp was more than twice what the Alpine had and, at 9.5-seconds 0–60 mph, it was nearly twice as quick. The live-rear-axle and four-speed gear-box were Ford's, but the chassis was Alpine's modified by Shelby with a stiffer suspension and rack-and-pinion steering. Brakes remained front discs and rear drums. Handling, roadholding, and ride comfort earned high marks, though the skinny tires and torquey V-8 added up to axle hop and poor traction off the line.

At $3499, the Tiger found 6495 buyers before an improved Tiger II went on sale in 1967. It had Ford's 289-cid V-8 rated at 200 hp and badges that read "Sunbeam V-8" instead of "Powered by Ford 260." Zero–60 times fell two seconds and top speed rose five mph. Most Cobra speed equipment could be fitted, including dual four-barrel carbs for up to 300 hp. Tigers were production-class road-racing threats in America and rally winners in Europe. On the street, they were significantly quicker than the last of the big Healeys or the first of Triumph's six-cylinder TRs. But it didn't matter. Chrysler had bought into the Rootes group in 1964 and couldn't countenance a Ford-powered car. The Tiger II was unceremoniously dumped during 1967.

Sunbeam Tiger II
1967

Wheelbase, in. 86.0

Weight, lbs. 2600

Price $3797

Engine ohv V-8

Displacement liters/cu. in. 4.7/289

Fuel system 1 x 2 bbl. carburetor

Horsepower @ rpm 200 @ 4400

Torque @ rpm 282 @ 2400

Transmission 4-speed manual

Performance

0–60 mph, sec. 7.5

Top speed, mph 122

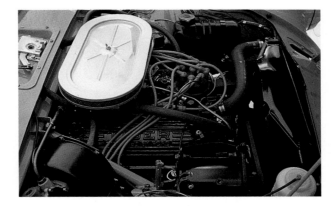

Nearly lost in the shadow of the omnipotent AC/Shelby Cobras was another Ford V-8-powered British roadster, the Sunbeam Tiger. It didn't have the back-alley brawler looks of the Corba, and never had as much power, but was by far the more comfortable everyday sports car. The Tiger didn't get the big 427- or 428-cid V-8s, but did share the small-block Cobra's 260- and 289-cid engines. Their horsepower in the Sunbeam was 164 and 200, respectively. That was less than in the Cobras, but still made for a lively and tractable sports car, especially in tandem with their Shelby-modified suspension and steering. Sunbeams also proved their mettle on the racetrack, where they enjoyed much production-class success. The Tiger's fate was sealed when Chrysler bought Sunbeam's parent company and, unwilling to have a Ford-powered car in its stable, killed the V-8 roadster in 1967.

TOYOTA 2000GT

*I*t was as good a 2.0-liter sports car as any automaker could offer. Coming from a Japanese manufacturer with no sporting tradition, the Toyota 2000GT was simply astonishing.

Toyota had been building cars for 30 years, but they'd been mundane people-movers of high reliability, little sophistication, and no soul. A world-class Grand Touring automobile would do wonders for its image. The solution started as a sports-car prototype built by Yamaha for Toyota's rival, Nissan. Heavily involved in the design was Count Albrecht Goertz, who had shaped the BMW 507. When Nissan turned down the prototype, Yamaha sold it to Toyota, which, after some slight changes, unveiled it at the 1965 Tokyo Motor Show as the 2000GT. Sales began in 1967.

Outsized driving lights beneath awkward pop-up headlamps distinguished the nose, but the aluminum-bodied two-seat hatchback was otherwise a fresh blend of familiar elements. The steel backbone chassis and independent suspension were inspired by the Lotus Elan. Rack-and-pinion steering, four-wheel disc brakes (the first on a Japanese production car), and magnesium-alloy road wheels were *de rigueur* in Europe but unheard of in an Asian.

Power came from a Yamaha-developed 2.0-liter dohc conversion of the 2.3-liter sohc inline-six from Toyota's big Crown sedan.

The interior had decent room for two American-sized adults, though just 4.8 cubic feet of luggage space. Equipment, however, was luxurious for a sports car of the day: full instrumentation in a rosewood dashboard, a modern heating/ventilating system, self-seeking AM radio, "rally" clock/stopwatch, telescopic steering wheel, a comprehensive tool kit.

Low production precluded volume sales at a reasonable price, but the car was the image-maker Toyota desired. Acceleration was very good for the available power, and overall behavior was superb. "When it comes to ride and handling, nobody in his right mind could need or want more in a road vehicle than the 2000GT has to offer," said *Road & Track* in June 1967. Prototypes did well in Japanese sports-car races, and Carroll Shelby's competition group developed three 2000GTs into 250-hp SCCA C-production winners. For good measure, a couple of convertibles were run off for the James Bond film *You Only Live Twice*. Overall, though, the 2000GT was just a bit ahead of its time: The world was not quite ready for a Japanese GT at Jaguar prices.

The comely-but-expensive 2000GT presaged an era of fine Japanese sports cars. It appeared in 1965 with independent suspension, four-wheel discs, and a gritty twincam 2.0-liter four. Just 337 were made.

Toyota 2000GT
1965–1970

Wheelbase, in. 91.7

Weight, lbs. 2480

Price $6800

Engine dohc I-6

Displacement liters/cu. in. 2.0/121

Fuel system 3 x 2 bbl. carburetors

Horsepower @ rpm 150 @ 6600

Torque @ rpm 130 @ 5000

Transmission 5-speed manual

Performance

0–60 mph, sec. 10.0

Top speed, mph 128

TOYOTA MR2

With its snappy handling, gemlike gearbox, and enchanting engine, Japan's first mid-engine production automobile didn't feel like an amalgam of off-the-shelf parts. But this corporate kit car was from Toyota, which drew on excellent components and knew how to use them.

MR2 means "Mid/Rear engine 2-seat." It went on sale in the U.S. in 1985 as an early '86 model, but was born in the late 1970s with Toyota looking for sports-car possibilities in existing hardware. When its popular Corolla sedan was reengineered for front-wheel drive, it had the building blocks. Corolla's transverse four-cylinder engine and transaxle were lifted and put midships in a unitized coupe hull; the same car's front strut suspension and disc brakes were used at both ends. All U.S.-market MR2s had the twincam version of the 1.6 liter first seen in the rear-drive Corolla GT-S coupe. Steering was rack-and-pinion and didn't need power assist, given the front/rear weight distribution of 44/56 percent.

Critics disliked the styling, but the MR2 was a model of efficient packag-

ing and satisfied that vital sports-car criteria by being no larger or heavier than necessary. Its cabin was snug but surprisingly airy and loaded with practical standard features, such as tilt steering and power mirrors. Leather, air conditioning, and power windows were options.

Few modern cars made their drivers smile so much. The engine loved to rev—it had to for best performance—but was so smooth and willing and the shifter so quick and precise. (*Car and Driver* in 1986 tabbed the MR2's gearbox and ergonomic layout as the world's best.) Noise levels were reasonable and the car was eminently tossable, with dreaded mid-engine oversteer surfacing only at racetrack cornering speeds. All that and Toyota reliability, no wonder the first MR2s sold at over sticker. When demand cooled, Toyota tempted the fickle market with optional automatic transmission, removable T-tops, a spoiler package, and for 1988, a supercharged model that had 145 hp and did 0–60 mph in seven seconds. Low mass and low cost, high fun and high quality, cars like the original "Mr. Two" don't often surface, much less emerge hot to trot right from the parts bin.

Toyota proved it could rearrange off-the-shelf components into an "exotic" mid-engine mix and come up with a great little sports car. The first MR2 wasn't really pretty, but it was plucky. Its twincam engine loved to rev, worked through a sublime gearbox, and teamed with wonderfully nimble independent suspension. Supercharged models were faster but not any more fun.

Toyota MR2
1985–1989

Wheelbase, in. 91.3

Weight, lbs. 2396

Price $10,999

Engine dohc I-4

Displacement liters/cu. in. 1.6/97

Fuel system Fuel injection

Horsepower @ rpm 112 @ 6600

Torque @ rpm 97 @ 4800

Transmission 5-speed manual

Performance

0–60 mph, sec. 8.1

Top speed, mph 121

TOYOTA MR2 TURBO

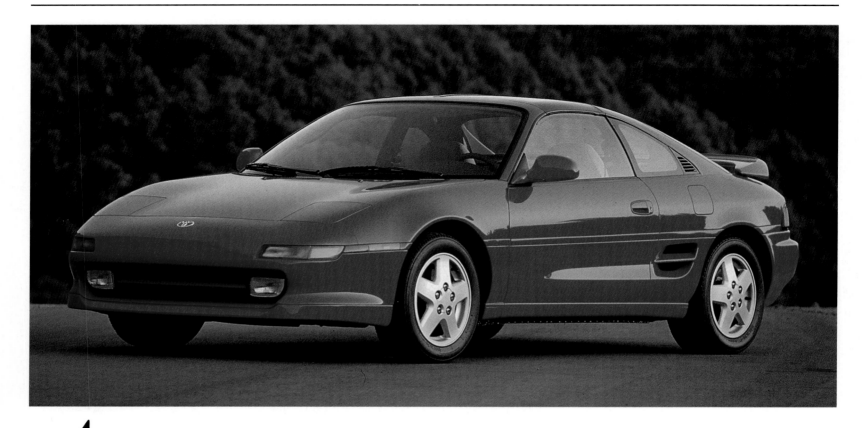

*A*n odd thing happened to the MR2 on its way to becoming a budget supercar. Oh, it had great performance and styling suitable for a Lamborghini, but gone was the sweet feet of the original. The second generation MR2 aspired to be more than a cheerful little sports car, and it somehow turned out less than the sum of its impressive parts.

Toyota laid plans for "Mr. Two" two during the bubbly 1980s, when the market for expensive—and profitable—sports cars seemed bright. Thus, the redesigned MR2 released for 1991 (there was no 1990 model) had more of everything. There was 3.2 inches more wheelbase for more cockpit space, 8.7 inches more body length for a roomier rear trunk, and curb weight increased more than 400 lbs. Its dohc four-cylinder engines also had more horsepower: 135 for the 2.2-liter base unit, and 200 for the uplevel choice, now a turbocharged and intercooled 2.0. Torque increased 40 percent. ABS was a new option, and the rear tires were now wider than the fronts. The more-luxurious interior featured a driver-side air bag.

It was the Turbo that best mimicked a supercar, with its sleek mid-engine design, beckoning 7000-rpm redline, and sophisticated mechanical air. But the engineers had miscalculated. The new car was treacherous in fast, hard cornering. Sudden oversteer, present only at the very limit in the first generation MR2, now came more easily, especially to the powerful Turbo. The '93s got significant rear-suspension revisions, wider-still rear tires, and, for good measure, larger, stronger brakes.

Toyota could fix the handling, but was powerless against the yen. Base prices in 1991 were a reasonable $14,898 for the standard model and $18,228 for the Turbo, but by '95, it had ballooned to $24,000 and near $30,000. This in a nervous economy and amid insurers hostile to two-seaters. U.S. sales that topped 14,000 in calendar '91 shriveled to 387 for 1995. There was no '96 model.

The second-generation MR2 had combined exotic-car credentials with Toyota reliability, but few mourned its passing. "Somehow a critical ingredient has been lost in the recipe," wrote Brock Yates in a *Car and Driver* review of the '93 model. ". . .[C]all it soul . . . For all its mechanical sophistication, the MR2 remains mysteriously tepid . . . Try as we might, our enthusiasm lags."

Toyota MR2 Turbo
1991–1996

Wheelbase, in. 94.5

Weight, lbs. 2915

Price $27,588

Engine Turbo dohc I-4

Displacement liters/cu. in. 2.0/122

Fuel system Fuel injection

Horsepower @ rpm 200 @ 6000

Torque @ rpm 200 @ 3200

Transmission 5-speed manual

Performance

0–60 mph, sec. 6.3

Top speed, mph 142

For the second-generation MR2, Toyota refocused its mid-engine two-seater from bewitching little sports car to junior exotic. The results were mixed. The styling had Ferrari overtones, the Turbo version made a supercar-like 100 hp per liter, and cabin comfort and overall assembly quality were far better than in most high-buck Europeans. But the car lacked the playful personality of the original "Mr. Two," and its tendency to surprise over-steer in a corner wasn't cured until well into production. Still, even with prices inflated by currency fluctuations, the MR2 Turbo was an unexpected taste of exotica.

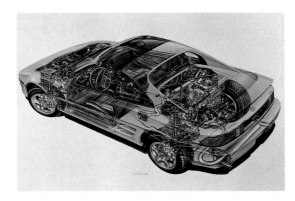

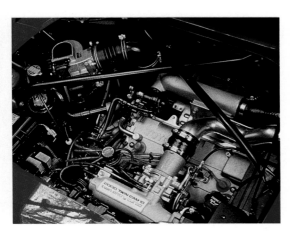

TOYOTA SUPRA TURBO

*T*oyota's new Supra bowed just as the market for high-buck Japanese sports cars collapsed. Sales dragged at 2000–3000 per year, making it almost as rare as some European exotics. Low volume wasn't all Supra had in common with a Ferrari, though. Its Turbo model performed like one.

Originally an upgraded Celica sporty coupe, Supra became its own rear-drive model when Celica went front-wheel drive for 1986. Settled comfortably into the role of a sound 2+2 GT, that version lasted though 1992. For '93, Supra was reborn as a costlier, more powerful 2+2 coupe. Styling, done in Japan, was rounded and more aggressive, with nods to the Ferrari F40 in the grille opening and bodyside intakes (they did not duct to the brakes). It even had a big basket-handle spoiler, a $420 Turbo option said to provide 66 lbs of downforce at 90 mph.

Although still a sizable sports car, the new Supra was smaller than its predecessor, with 1.8 inches less wheelbase and 4.2 inches less body length. To save weight, Toyota rejected such items as dual exhaust tips, and even specified hollow-fiber carpeting. Supra rode a shortened, modified Lexus SC300 platform and shared the luxury coupe's engine. Here it had 220 hp in base form and 320 in the Turbo, which used one turbocharger for low-rpm boost, kicked in a second above 4500 rpm, and then ran both to make an impressive 106.8 hp per liter. The cabin was austere for the price and the rear seats were mere parcel bins, but everything else was in place: dual air bags, traction control, a removable aluminum roof panel.

A flick of the wrist shifted the Getrag six-speed, and the well-sorted suspension and magnificent ABS disc brakes kept the car composed even in the wildest maneuvers, with only a harsh bad-pavement ride dimming the picture. The Turbo begged comparison to the world's best. *Car and Driver* chose it over the Mazda RX-7, Nissan 300ZX Turbo, and Porsche 968. *Road & Track* in August '93 pit it against the $189,500 Ferrari 512TR and $99,000 Porsche 911 Turbo. The Toyota was a blink slower to 60 mph, but gripper in corners, faster through the slalom, and stopped shorter from 60 mph. "Suspend your preconceptions, forget the legends, erase the tallies of ancient race wins," said the editors, who judged the Turbo Supra an "exotic" in all but one vital intangible. Call it "the builder's courage to express his work uncompromisingly," said *R&T*, which found indecision in Supra's styling. But if launching—and sustaining—an expensive Japanese sports car in a hostile market isn't courage, then what is?

Toyota Supra Turbo
1993–

Wheelbase, in. 100.4

Weight, lbs. 3480

Price $41,000

Engine Twin turbo dohc I-6

Displacement liters/cu. in. 3.0/183

Fuel system Fuel injection

Horsepower @ rpm 320 @ 5600

Torque @ rpm 315 @ 4000

Transmission 6-speed manual

Performance

0–60 mph, sec. 5.0

Top speed, mph 154

The second-generation Supra was born of an optimistic time when the demand for very fast, high-tech Japanese sports cars looked insatiable. But the market changed, killing the RX-7, 300ZX, and MR2, and crippling the NSX. But the Supra soldiers on, and in Turbo form, matches some European exotics in performance, if not price or prestige. Using two turbochargers in sequence, Supra's twincam inline-six pumps 320 hp to wide rear wheels. The quick-shifting six-speed manual is preferred by sporting drivers over the four-speed automatic, but with either, the excellent suspension and resolute ABS disc brakes make for near-faultless control in most any maneuver. The cabin is an inviting place for two; the rear seats are really parcel bins. Some critics say the styling lacks cohesion. The bodyside scoops are decorative and although the rear spoiler looks pretentious, Toyota says it's functional. Projector-beam headlights (bottom right) provide illumination suitable to the Supra Turbo's speed potential.

TRIUMPH TR2

*F*or an early-'50s sports car, the TR2 was a revelation. Not only did it offer fine performance, good fuel economy, and modern styling, it cost little more than an MG and far less than a Jaguar—not bad for Triumph's first true sports car.

Triumph of Coventry built motorcycles and cyclecars before turning to proper automobiles in 1923. By the mid-1930s, it was selling lush sports-tourers that did well in international rallying. Then the Depression forced the firm into liquidation, leaving Sir John Black's Standard Motor Car Company to acquire Triumph's automotive business in 1944.

Black envied MG's growing export success, but had failed in a bid to buy Morgan, so he ordered up his own sports car for Triumph. A 1952 prototype, the 20TS ("TR1"), looked promising but needed more work, so engineers Harry Webster and Ken Richardson devised a sturdy new frame to replace the original '30s-era chassis, plus an improved "wet liner" version of the over-head-valve four from Standard's 1949 Vanguard sedan. Longtime Triumph designer Walter Belgrove added a longer rear end that worked beautifully

with the prototype's smooth nose, integral fenders, and cutaway doors.

Logically named TR2, the new sporting Triumph was warmly received on its 1953 debut. Few contemporary cars offered 100-mph performance for so little money (just under $2500)—nor up to 26 miles per U.S. gallon when driven with restraint. Although the ride was harsh, handling a bit crude, and the cockpit typically two-seater tight, the TR2 was miles more modern than a T-Series MG. It even acquired a "competition proved" aura when a special streamliner ran 120 mph on Belgium's famed Jabaekke Highway. Production was slow to get rolling—just 250 cars in all of '53—but improvements came quickly. By 1954, Triumph was offering extra-cost wire wheels, electric overdrive, radial tires, even a lift-off hardtop.

With all this, plus inestimable British charm, the TR2 heralded Triumph as a sports-car force to be reckoned with. Even the new 1953 Austin-Healey 100 couldn't dim its luster, for the Triumph was cheaper, if a bit less elegant. It was far from perfect, of course, but a legend had been born, and Triumph began nurturing it with the improved TR3 of 1955.

Triumph's first true sports car, the TR2, looked more modern than the contemporary MG TF and cost far less than a Jaguar, yet could top 100 mph. It used body-on-frame construction and a suspension that employed coil springs and wishbones in front and a live axle on leaf springs in back. Ride and handling were nothing special, but the TR2 had a tough simplicity that endeared it to owners and turned a legion of Americans into sports-car fans and Triumph lovers. Total production was 8628 during the model's three-year run. This example has the optional lift-off hardtop.

TRIUMPH TR3A

*B*efore there could be a TR3A, there had to be a TR3. Well, for everyone except Triumph, which never officially applied any suffix letters to these cars—or to the later TR3B. But distinctions are necessary for discussion, and they've long been part of TR lore.

We should also note that the TR3 went through two phases. The first involved the 1955–56 models, which were distinguished from the TR2 by a flush-set eggcrate grille. Modified ports and larger carbs (still twin SUs) added 5 hp to give the 2.0-liter four-cylinder 95. Five more came by an interim switch in cylinder heads after the first 3300 engines, from the introductory "LeMans" casting to a "high port" design.

"Phase 2" began with the '57 models, which became the first series-built British cars with standard front disc brakes. Triumph also improved the rear drums and substituted a sturdier back axle, still leaf-sprung. Coil springs and double wishbones continued for the independent front suspension. Also new was a so-called GT Kit. Aimed at rallying's Sports and GT classes, this option merely delivered the factory lift-off hardtop and outside door handles.

Those handles became standard with the TR3A, which bowed for 1958 wearing a rather Detroit-inspired "wide mouth" grille, plus a locking trunk handle and modified headlamps; sturdier bumpers were less obvious. Although sales were better than ever, Triumph was working on a more stylish sports car that would materialize in 1961 as the TR4. Perhaps as a preview, the new model's upsized 2.1-liter engine became available for TR3As starting in 1959, though apparently few were installed.

However, Triumph found itself with a surplus of TR3As by 1961, the result of misjudged market demand and overproduction. Happily, the firm's U.S. distributor wasn't that sure of the new TR4, and, deciding to hedge its bets, offered to dispose of leftover TR3As. The result was an American-market conversion, the TR3B, with slightly nicer appointments and the TR4's new all-synchro gearbox. All but 500 also received the 2.1 engine.

As it happened, the U.S. took to the TR4 in a big way, so after seven years, the TR3 generation was honorably retired in October 1962. It had done a remarkable job. The TR4 would do an even better one.

The TR3 appeared for 1955 as an upgraded TR2 and was even more successful than its predecessor, with 74,945 built over the series' seven-year run. Early differences from the TR2 ran to a new grille and five hp more for the 2.0-liter four. For '57, the TR3 became the first British production car with front disc brakes. The example pictured is a TR3A, which bowed for '58 with a wide-mouth grille, modified headlamps, a locking trunk, sturdier bumpers, and another five hp. Its sales topped 58,000 and the U.S. distributor, going with a proven commodity, stalled importation of its TR4 successor. It instead conjured up a U.S.-market only TR3B; 3331 of these were made and most had the TR4's 100-hp 2.1-liter engine and all-synchro gearbox.

Triumph TR3A
1958–1961

Wheelbase, in. 88.0

Weight, lbs. 2050

Price $2750

Engine ohv I-4

Displacement liters/cu. in. 2.0/122

Fuel system 2 x 1 bbl. carburetors

Horsepower @ rpm 100 @ 5000

Torque @ rpm 117 @ 3000

Transmission 4-speed manual

Performance

0–60 mph, sec. 12.5

Top speed, mph 102

TRIUMPH TR4A

*I*mproved old wine in a nice new bottle aptly describes the Triumph TR4. The chassis, for example, came from the TR2/TR3, though handling was improved by three-inch wider tracks and a switch from antique cam-and-lever steering to more precise rack-and-pinion. Up front was a 2.1-liter four that owed much to the sturdy 2.0-liter engine of previous TRs. The same held for the four-speed manual gearbox, though a synchronized first gear struck a blow for modernity.

That left a new slab-sided body as the main attraction. Designed by Italian Giovanni Michelotti, it looked rather masculine despite a softly curved front with full-width grille and distinctive "eyelid" headlamps. *Road & Track* contended that on "strictly practical grounds, there is no disputing the worth of the new bodywork. [The] squared-off stern provides space for a relatively large luggage locker, and a couple of much-needed inches of width have been added to the interior. The coming of true civilization was most apparent in the provision of rollup side windows." The soft top, alas, remained a time-consuming complexity, but in-dash ventilation was a first for a British car, and the optional lift-off

hardtop now had a replaceable canvas section that made for a "surrey" roof, a sort of early targa idea.

Inevitably, the TR4 was heavier and a bit slower than late TR3s, and stiff springing continued to give a rock-hard ride and some unwanted bump-steer. But Triumph had a fix for the latter: independent rear suspension, via coil springs and semitrailing links. It arrived in 1965 for a revised TR4A that also featured a permanently attached soft top that was much easier to operate. Although the new rear end tended to bottom easily, it improved handling and ride comfort, especially on rough surfaces. No wonder the independent suspension quickly went from optional to standard equipment.

The 4A only enhanced the Triumph that had impressed *Road & Track* as offering "excellent performance at moderate initial cost . . . [A] sporting driver would search for a long time to beat the combination." Still, time waits for no car, and rivals were beginning to beat the TR4 on several fronts by 1968. But Triumph had a fix for that too, and it's in this book: the TR6.

**Triumph TR4A
1965–1967**

Wheelbase, in. 88.0

Weight, lbs. 2240

Price $2900

Engine ohv I-6

Displacement liters/cu. in. 2.1/130

Fuel system 2 x 1 bbl. carburetors

Horsepower @ rpm 109 @ 4700

Torque @ rpm 128 @ 3350

Transmission 4-speed manual

Performance

0–60 mph, sec. 10.9

Top speed, mph 105

It may have been little more than a rebodied TR3, but it was that attractive new body, by Italian Giovanni Michelotti, that made the TR4 special. It bowed for 1961 with a roomier cockpit, rollup windows, a wider track, rack-and-pinion steering, and the 100-hp 2.1. Triumph built 40,253 before moving on for 1965 with the TR4A. This one got a better soft top and a bump to 109 hp, but more importantly, made available a coil-sprung independent rear suspension. Ride and handling were greatly improved. Pictured is one of the 28,465 TR4As produced through 1967.

TRIUMPH SPITFIRE

*T*he Triumph Spitfire was the Mazda Miata of the '60s: a simple, appealing, yet fairly practical sports car that was also cheap thanks to heavy use of high-volume family-car components. Of course, being a Japanese invention for the '90s, the Miata boasts workmanship and reliability this British car never knew, yet it's significant that Mazda kept a Spitfire around when developing the Miata.

Named for Britain's renowned World War II fighter plane, the Spitfire was Triumph's answer to other budget sports cars of the early '60s, especially the MG Midget and Austin-Healey Sprite. It was a bit larger and roomier than those rivals, and more sophisticated with its all-independent suspension versus a solid back axle. Both the suspension and the 1.1-liter engine came from Triumph's small Herald line, but another 12 hp was persuaded from the all-iron four, and the suspension went onto a unique new backbone chassis with a shorter wheelbase than the Herald's.

Styling, by Triumph's Italian *maestro* Giovanni Michelotti, was pert, even pretty. As on the Herald and the early "bugeye" Sprite, a one-piece

hood/fenders assembly tilted up from the front to give unrivaled engine access.

The Spitfire was reasonably quick for its modest price—but quite a handful in hard corners. The reason was the simple swing-axle rear suspension, which was prone to easy wheel tuck-under that made for sudden, usually alarming, oversteer. Ralph Nader apparently never noticed, though, and it didn't deter buyers, especially in the U.S. In fact, by British standards, the Spitfire was a big hit almost from the start. Sales were strong for the better part of 18 years despite reduced performance and numerous ill-advised changes after 1970, although the dreaded oversteer was long tamed by then. That lifespan encompassed Mark 2, 3, IV, and "1500" evolutions, although most enthusiasts believe the Mark 3 was the last really good Spitfire in the original mold.

A Spitfire can still charm like few other cars regardless of price. Like the Miata it helped inspire, this "junior TR" contrives somehow to be more than the sum of its parts, and that's a rare sort of magic indeed.

Arguably the best of the scaled-down sports cars was the Triumph Spitfire. Though the all-independent suspension was flawed by ill-mannered swing rear axles, pert styling and 90-mph capability helped Triumph sell 45,753 Mark I editions like this one. All told, 314,332 Spitfires were built through 1980, but their allure diminished with each series after about 1970.

Triumph Spitfire Mark 1
1962–1965

Wheelbase, in. 83.0

Weight, lbs. 1570

Price $2000

Engine ohv I-4

Displacement liters/cu. in. 1.1/70

Fuel system 1 x 2 bbl. carburetor

Horsepower @ rpm 63 @ 5750

Torque @ rpm 67 @ 3500

Transmission 4-speed manual

Performance

0–60 mph, sec. 16.5

Top speed, mph 92

TRIUMPH GT6 MARK 3

*I*f the Spitfire was fun with a four, reasoned enthusiasts, it should be dynamite with a six. Oddly, Triumph resisted the idea, straining as it was to meet Spitfire demand. But the little roadster had evolved from the Herald sedan, which had a six-cylinder version called Vitesse. So Triumph finally answered its public's pleas with a "big-inch" Spitfire, the GT6.

It arrived in 1966 as essentially a six-cylinder Spitfire with a fixed fastback roof that made some people think "junior Jaguar E-type." The tin-top transformation was handled by consultant Giovanni Michelotti, but was patterned after the factory Spitfire GT fastbacks that raced in 1963 and '64. Triumph's 2.0-liter straight-six fit easily beneath the Spitfire bonnet, and mated to a new all-synchro gearbox. Suspension was firmed up to handle 95 hp, and the cockpit was spruced up from that of the concurrent Spitfire Mark 2.

Though the GT6 shared the Spit's quirky swing-axle rear end, it was far less prone to oversteer, perhaps because it had some extra weight at the back. And starting at just over $3000, it was a good value. *Road & Track* judged it a fine effort overall, "smooth, [with] good torque,

low noise level, and agility as well as stability in its handling . . . [The GT6] has no parallel and it's worth the money."

For 1968, came a GT6 Mark 2—GT6+ in America—with a raised "bone-in-mouth" front bumper, revamped dash, flow-through ventilation, and a rear suspension cleverly reworked to provide double-wishbone geometry for no-sweat cornering behavior. Power was unchanged for the U.S., but rose to 104 elsewhere via a new cylinder head and freer-breathing exhaust. A Mark 3 arrived for all markets in 1971, bearing crisp new Michelotti tail styling *a la* the contemporary Spitfire Mark IV, plus various detail updates. Unfortunately, strangling emissions standards reduced U.S. horsepower to 90, which then slumped to just 79.

But sales were falling, too, and with the first energy crisis providing an excuse for euthanasia, the GT6 was killed after 1973. Yet it remained eminently likeable right to the end. As *R&T* noted in 1969: "Where else can you get a . . . 100+ mph coupe with a proper chassis, good finish and jazzy looks for $3000?" Happily, that's still the going rate for even the nicest GT6s. Sports-car bargain-hunters, take note.

Take a Spitfire, add a fastback roof, and install a six-cylinder and the result is the Triumph GT6. The engine was Triumph's own 2.0-liter and fit as well in the Spitfire chassis as it did in the company's Herald sedan, which formed the basis for the Spitfire. The 1966 debut version retained the deficient swing-axle rear suspension, but a Mark 2 evolution for '68 got improved rear underpinnings that cured handling problems and up to 104 hp. The Mark 3 appeared for 1971 with revised tail styling but with the same hatchback roofline. In America, Triumph's main market, the Mark 3 started with 90 hp then sunk under emissions rules to just 79. Sales fell, too, and the fastback Spitfire was shelved after 1973.

Triumph GT6 Mark 3
1971–1973

Wheelbase, in. 83.0

Weight, lbs. 1975

Price $3250

Engine ohv I-6

Displacement liters/cu. in. 2.0/122

Fuel system 2 x 1 bbl. carburetors

Horsepower @ rpm 90 @ 4700

Torque @ rpm 117 @ 3400

Transmission 5-speed manual

Performance

0–60 mph, sec. 12.0

Top speed, mph 100

TRIUMPH TR6

*I*t was no Austin-Healey 3000, but the TR6 was a good substitute for those seeking a traditional "big six" British roadster with a masculine image.

The TR6 was a follow-up to the 1967–68 TR5 PI, which was basically a TR4A with a torquey pushrod six instead of a four. PI meant "petrol injection," newly applied to extract 150 hp from the elderly 2.5-liter engine. But Triumph's fuel-injection system somehow ran afoul of U.S. emissions standards, so Americans got a similar TR250 model with a detoxed twin-carburetor engine making only 104 hp.

That setup was used for the TR6, which bowed in early '69. The TR4A-origin body got a new look thanks to Karmann of Germany and it was a very effective facelift, with a trendy chopped-off Kamm tail, a longer hood, and a prominent wide-mouth grille. The accessory hardtop also was revamped, gaining a more angular look and orthodox one-piece construction.

Road & Track found in its $3400 1971 TR6 test car a "distinctive combination of qualities at a reasonable price . . . with ride and han-

dling far from outstanding and a somewhat cramped cockpit but . . . an excellent 6-cyl. engine, luxurious finish and trimmings, and a roadster top that's easy to put up and down." The editors also had "no question" about reliability and durability, but they were writing well before Japanese cars began redefining those terms.

The TR6 lasted some seven years with few interim changes. Among the more important were a reprofiled camshaft giving a smoother idle and better low-speed tractability, plus an updated version of the optional Laycock electric overdrive; both appeared in early '73. Far less welcome were the big and ugly black bumper guards that sprouted on 1973–74 U.S. models, a necessary response to new five-mph impact standards. Still, the big TR aged gracefully.

But it couldn't last forever, and the old soldier faded away in mid-1976. By that time, troubled British Leyland Corporation had introduced a TR7 that would generate nowhere near as much affection—or sales—as the TR6. It was one of many mistakes that would ultimately cost British Leyland its life.

Triumph TR6
1969–1976

Wheelbase, in. 88.0

Weight, lbs. 2475

Price $3500

Engine ohv I-6

Displacement liters/cu. in. 2.5/152

Fuel system 2 x 1 bbl. carburetors

Horsepower @ rpm 106 @ 4900

Torque @ rpm 142 @ 3000

Transmission 4-speed manual

Performance

0–60 mph, sec. 10.7

Top speed, mph 109

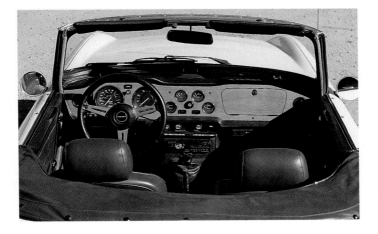

One British writer called the TR6 "the last of the hairy-chested mass-produced sports cars." That's accurate, if one considers that the TR6 was compared, usually unfavorably, to the first of the new-era sports cars, the Datsun 240Z. The Z had more more elan and quality, but the TR6 had enough brawny presence to satisfy 94,600 buyers over its respectably long lifetime. Muscular styling, with squared shoulders and big wheel openings, fueled its image. So did the hidebound but wonderfully torquey ohv inline-six. Sports cars would never again blend simplicity and toughness in quite this way.

TRIUMPH TR8

*B*e careful what you draw, it might become a car. That's what happened with the Triumph TR7 and its V-8 sibling, the TR8.

In the early 1970s, British Leyland was eyeing a new sports car to replace those of its member marques, the Triumph TR6 and the MGB. Just for fun, stylist Harris Mann doodled a sort of bubbletop wedge with a big upswept curve on the bodysides. Somehow, management saw this design and deemed it perfect for the new two-seater. Others didn't. After walking around the TR7 on its 1975 debut, Italian master stylist Giorgetto Giugiaro eyed the bodyside sculpting and lamented: "Oh, no! They've done it on *this* side too!"

Unlike the TR6, the TR7 was first sold only as a coupe, used a beam axle rather than independent rear suspension, and had a 2.0-liter overhead-cam four instead of a pushrod six. A four-speed gearbox was standard, but a new five-speed was optional in lieu of electric overdrive. A three-speed automatic also was available.

Being relatively wide, the TR7 had a roomy cockpit and a broad stance that contributed to stable handling. It also had room for the 3.5-liter V-8 from corporate cousin Rover and that's what went into the TR8 that bowed as a 1980 model. The TR8 also got firmer damping, standard power steering, and nicer trim.

Unfortunately, both these Triumphs suffered mediocre workmanship and erratic production that only accelerated BL's fast-falling fortunes. Convertibles were added in 1979 with hopes of improving sales. Arguably prettier than the coupes, the ragtops were also far more flexible—enough that parking on shallow inclines could twist the unitized hull sufficiently to prevent opening the doors. Despite all this, BL built more than 112,000 TR7s, but only 2497 TR8s, of which 2308 were U.S. models (including just 202 coupes).

Though pleasant and satisfyingly quick when working right, the TR8 was too little too late. By the time it arrived, BL was on the ropes, and the firm's 1980 British government takeover left no future for any TR—or MGB, or Triumph Spitfire. BL has since become the privately held Rover Group, which has a dandy new sports car in the MGF. That leaves the TR8 to be mourned as the last sporting Triumph and a promise unfulfilled.

The TR7 and TR8 were British Leyland's version of a modern Triumph sports car. The TR7 had an 86-hp (105 in Europe) 2.0-liter four and a 9.1-second 0–60 mph time. The TR8 used a 3.5-liter Rover V-8 and was satisfyingly faster. Handling was good and the wide cockpit comfortable, but with a solid-axle rear, subpar quality, and debatable styling, neither did justice to the Triumph legacy.

Triumph TR8
1980–1981

Wheelbase, in. 85.0

Weight, lbs. 2655

Price $11,500

Engine ohv V-8

Displacement liters/cu. in. 3.5/215

Fuel system 2 x 1 bbl. carburetors

Horsepower @ rpm 133 @ 5000

Torque @ rpm 165 @ 3200

Transmission 5-speed manual

Performance

0–60 mph, sec. 8.5

Top speed, mph 133

TVR GRIFFITH

TVR is one of those tiny British automakers that's managed to survive its own checkered history. Established by Trevor (TreVoR) Wilkinson in 1954, it quickly turned from kit cars to an odd-looking fiberglass-bodied coupe, the Grantura. Also sold fully assembled, the Grantura had a multi-tube backbone chassis designed to accept a variety of proprietary engines and suspension components. But sales were difficult, and TVR was reorganized no fewer than three times by the early '60s.

Then, a break. Three Granturas ran at Sebring in 1962, and two of the drivers happened to maintain their personal cars—a Grantura and a Shelby Cobra—at the New York shops of Jack Griffith. Griffith's crew wondered if the Cobra's 289 Ford V-8 fit the TVR. It did. Seeing the potential, Griffith asked TVR to supply Granturas for Stateside installation of the Cobra drivetrain. Desperate for cash, TVR agreed, and the TVR Griffith went on sale in 1963.

Drivetrain apart, the new model was a Mark 3 Grantura with stronger, wider wire wheels. The hood was bulged to clear the V-8, which Griffith offered in stock 195-hp form or 271-hp "Hi Performance" tune. The only gearbox was a Ford-built four-speed. Like all early TVRs, the Griffith had little cockpit or luggage space, a very hard ride, and typically casual "cottage" workmanship. The original 200 model also tended to overheat, but a better-engineered 400 replaced it in spring 1964, bringing twin thermostatic cooling fans that addressed the problem but didn't entirely cure it. The 400 also introduced the sharply cropped tail and big rear window that would persist at TVR through the end of the '70s.

The 400 was well received, and TVR was soon shipping five engineless cars per week. High power and low weight meant vivid performance, but nose-heavy balance could make it a handling nightmare. The Griffith, said British auto writer Roger Bell, "has too much power for its own good in less than perfect conditions. That's what makes it so exciting . . ."

The car was soon done in by its own quality problems and, more seriously, a prolonged U.S. dockworkers strike. Jack Griffith gave up after 1965, thus shattering TVR's fragile finances and forcing the Blackpool concern into liquidation. While there'd be many more TVRs to come, none were quite as hairy as the original Griffith.

TVR Griffith
1963–1965

Wheelbase, in. 85.5

Weight, lbs. 1905

Price $4000

Engine ohv V-8

Displacement liters/cu. in. 4.7/289

Fuel system 1 x 4 bbl. carburetors

Horsepower @ rpm 271 @ 6500

Torque @ rpm 314 @ 2400/3400

Transmission 4-speed manual

Performance

0–60 mph, sec. 5.7

Top speed, mph 152

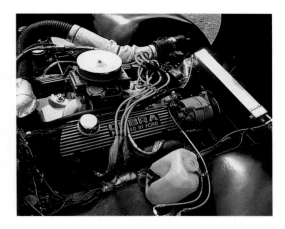

Small-time fabricator Trevor Wilkinson put some Detroit muscle into a slightly modified version of his fiberglass-body coupe for a wild sports-car hot rod. Based on the mild four-cylinder TVR Grantura, the Griffith used Ford's 289-cid V-8 and four-speed manual. The injection of power and front-end mass turned the little lightweight into a combative bantam that was fast and frightening. The 1965 Griffith 200 model pictured has typical, period-correct extras, including Ford "Cobra" engine hop-ups, a Hurst shift linkage, and Cragar mag wheels. About 300 TVR Griffiths were built.

VECTOR M12

Overhyped fantasy or serious supercar? The Vector is both proof that ideas are one thing, results quite another.

It was conceived as "aerospace technology for the street" by Gerry Wiegert, an industrial designer and sometime engineer. A mockup shown in 1976 attracted much attention with its wedgy, edgy styling and promises of 600 hp, composite body, and aircraft-quality construction. Encouraged, Wiegert formed Vehicle Design Force in Los Angeles to realize his mid-engine dream. Despite scant capital, a running prototype was completed by 1978, and Wiegert showed it everywhere possible to raise money for production, which would be handled by a new Vector Aeromotive Corporation. But funds were hard to come by and the engineering far from perfected. Still, the renamed Vector W8 Twin-Turbo got vast press coverage as a soon-to-be-available Ferrari-beater—and kept on getting it for more than 10 years.

In 1988, Wiegert took Vector Aeromotive public and raised $20 million. Although serious production finally seemed imminent, only 18 W8s were built and the company was suspiciously broke by 1995. Wiegert was ousted by his own stockholders, and Vector passed to

Indonesian-owned MegaTech Ltd., which soon bought Lamborghini and moved Vector to Florida.

Vector had prepared a show car, the Avtech SC (also known as the WX3), and the new operation used this to create a successor model, the M12. British designer Peter Stevens softened the styling and engineers junked the twin-turbo V-8 and costly "aerospace" technology for a Lamborghini Diablo V-12 and conventional construction. New facilities promised truly professional small-scale production at the rate of 150 or so per year.

Road & Track found the M12 "an elemental car, provoking that corner of the brain that prefers violence over mature negotiation." Although the test car was a "prototype hack," the magazine deemed workmanship competitive with anything from Italy. The M12 was more accommodating than the W8, yet no less a straightline rocket. As for handling, the M12 let *R&T*'s man "throw it any which way I liked. [But] the Vector is a huge car . . . and just guiding it through corners is a fairly intense achievement."

So the Vector is finally real after more than 20 years. The only question now is, how long can it last?

Vector M12
1996–

Wheelbase, in. 108.0

Weight, lbs. 3600

Price $184,000

Engine dohc V-12

Displacement liters/cu. in. 5.7/348

Fuel system Fuel injection

Horsepower @ rpm 490 @ 6800

Torque @ rpm 425 @ 5200

Transmission 5-speed manual

Performance

0–60 mph, sec. 4.8

Top speed, mph 190

Out of a checkered corporate past comes an American-bred mid-engine supercar. Vector was formed in the mid-1970s to build an exotic coupe that employed aerospace technology, styling inspired by the stealth fighter, and a twin-turbo V-8. Several iterations were manufactured, but none in any numbers. By 1995, Vector was in the hands of Lamborghini's Indonesian parent company and the M12 was a reality. The M12 retains the earlier Vectors' jackknife doors, but has—believe it or not—less outrageous styling. Power is from a Lamborghini V-12 also used in the Diablo. The car's intriguing, but Vector's long-term prognosis is far from decided.

INDEX